Turbulent School

by

Jeremy Shaw

Turbulent School

First published online
ISBN 978-1-68222-548

Second Edition © 2021 Jeremy Shaw
ISBN 978-1-912728-34-3

Illustrations and cover design by Miki Lane

Printed, published and distributed by
Quacks Books,
7 Grape Lane,
Petergate,
York YO1 7HU
01904 635967
design@quacks.info

Contents

Author's notes

The events described here occurred in four very different failing schools. Identifying features of teachers, pupils and places have been disguised and descriptions of the key players have been merged to protect their identities.

This novella is based on the author's blog, turbulentschool.net that was written during the Covid19 crisis. Many teachers were asking serious questions about levelling up: were examinations, league tables and Ofsted helpful or fair, given England's growing social inequalities?

Ofsted is an acronym, standing for the Office for Standards in Education. It carries out regular inspections of every state school in England. Originally, Ofsted Inspections were a week long, with two months to prepare. Now they occur at short notice. Schools used to be rated on a five-point scale, which included "requires improvement" as well as "inadequate". This was reduced to a four-point scale. Inadequate schools undergo 'special measures'.

From Thomas Hobbes' *Leviathan*

From this fundamental law of nature, by which men are commanded to endeavour peace, is derived this second law: that a man be willing, when others are so too, as far forth as for peace and defence of himself he shall think it necessary, to lay down this right to all things; and be contented with so much liberty against other men as he would allow other men against himself. For as long as every man holdeth this right, of doing anything he liketh; so long are all men in the condition of war. But if other men will not lay down their right, as well as he, then there is no reason for anyone to divest himself of his: for that were to expose himself to prey, which no man is bound to, rather than to dispose himself to peace.

Alphabetical Character List

Mr Appleby: father of Nicholas and Paul
Nicholas Appleby: Year 7 victim of bullying
Dr Adam Awad: Syrian refugee, previously vice principal of an international school
Trevor Black: Manager, Athletics Centre, Snowdonia
Enaya Blake: teacher in charge of Kev's special unit
Angela Clayton, a Teacher Governor and English Teacher, wife of John Clayton
Gerry Conlin: ex-pupil and drug dealer
Rowena Cross: RE teacher
Lee Doonan: nicknamed 'Cuckoo', a Year 9 truant
Sylvie Francome: a girl with cerebral palsy from Enaya Blake's Special Unit
Harry Green: under-18 runner
Jacob Hornsby: new Chair of Governors
Nathan James: freckle-faced prefect
Jo Johnson: Year 8 pupil with white hair and very fair skin
Archie Laud: Head of Science: previously Principal of a private school in the Gulf
Mrs Lawton: mother of Alice and Katie, parent governor at Eydon Vale
Alice Lawton: gifted Year 11 at Eydon Vale, who wants to go to Oxford
Katie Lawton: her sister, a forthright Year 7 pupil
Kylie Lawrence: Head of PE
Ming Lee: able Year 11 at Eydon Vale
Noha Malek: a gifted runner from Somalia
Peter McIntosh: new Assistant Head and Maths teacher
Hanif Megat HMI: perceptive, poetry loving but ruthless Ofsted Inspector
Gillian Newsome: able Year 11 at Eydon Vale
Pandora O'Connell: Year 11 comedienne and Mairead's younger sister
Milo O'Donnell: new Assistant Head and English Teacher
Elizabeth Oliphant: Head of Art
Sir Henry Robinson: Chair of Trustees
Iona Salomon HMI: Lead Ofsted Inspector:
Kev Samson: troubled boy with reading difficulties
Elroy Samson: Kev's older brother

Jake Sangster: Year 8 pupil, younger brother of Peter
Pete Sangster: bright but disruptive Year 11 pupil
Tom Shelton MP
John Silver: Head of Rectory Road School
Jonas Smith: traveller
Brian Smithson, the Assistant Head of Eydon Vale
Rhiannon Starr: Deputy Headteacher, then Acting Head of Eydon Vale
Maria Telemann: new History teacher
Alan Thurwell: asthmatic 60-year-old metalwork teacher, nicknamed 'Thor'
Elinor Tully: Head of Music
Patrick Wadsworth: disruptive Year 8 pupil with terminally ill grandfather
Jane Williams: bully/ victim: wears pigtails and plays piano
'Whiz' Wilson: new Australian Geography and PE teacher
Bea Wright: Northern Irish consultant on Guided Discipline
Tom Windsor: gifted speaker, temporally excluded for assaulting Peter McIntosh

Introduction

Moving to an almost exclusively white area like Holmesside was a mean business for me. When we lived in London, I used to be in the top set of an "outstanding" school. My younger brother Kev was always being suspended from his special school. When the Official at the Local Education Authority suggested there might be a place in Eydon Vale's special unit, my mother jumped at it, insisting I should go there to keep an eye on him.

All that summer, Kev and I heard the most gruesome stories about Eydon Vale. The kids round about went on and on about the bullying. Its reputation was the worst in town. No one did any work. The exam results were the pits. A teacher had been shot in the playground. There was even gossip about motorbikes being driven around the flat roof.

Apparently, one of the bad lads called Jake pulled the head teacher's beard. He and his crew would hang around the gates and single out the new kids. They would take them to the food bins and toss them in. Then the lids would go on. The new kids would have to lie all day in the dark in all that detritus. By the end of the summer holidays, Kev was nauseous.

The back-to-school shopping for pens, pencils and shoes made him feel even more anxious. He started having nightmares, which got so bad, he was afraid to go to sleep. The morning before term started, he threw up. My mother just gave him dry toast and told him not to worry. Everyone was the same. Starting a new school or a new job was hard. It was part of growing up, but he would get over it.

My mother made me walk Kev to school on that first day. The bullies would see Kev was my brother. No one would dare to lay a finger on him. On the first day of term, Kev came downstairs, rubbing the sleep from his eyes. My mother cracked a joke about the food bins. "Not funny!" I said. Off we went through the shadow of Eydon Vale's gates.

The kids had made Eydon Vale sound worse than Dracula's castle. But no one was lying in wait for Kev. Transferring from a special school to the unit made an extraordinary difference to him. This brief period has been the happiest in his life. He has developed a new sense of identity, his confidence improved, and he learned to read and write. Mrs Blake, the teacher in charge of the special unit, could not have been kinder or more professional.

(Extracts from "First Memories of School" by Elroy Samson.)

Chapter One: Ofsted

My own experience at Eydon Vale turned out to be as rewarding but almost as tragic as that of Elroy's brother, Kev. Life in a turbulent school was never easy, of course. Let me tell you what it feels like for a teacher in a turbulent school to be 'Ofsteded'. Imagine you are eating breakfast with your toddler. Someone with a clipboard enters your kitchen, finds an empty chair and starts taking notes. Excited by the extra attention, your baby starts throwing his porridge on the floor and smears it in his hair. Knowing that your whole career is on the line, you wince and try to carry on regardless, but your toddler picks up your anxiety. There is an unmistakable sound of a nappy being filled. Then the inspector leaves the room.

At the District Hospital on Holmesside, there is always a bed reserved for Ofsted casualties by the Psychiatric Consultant. For most teachers, especially those in England's wealthier areas, a school inspection just means a few sleepless nights, but in the worst cases, lives can be ruined and schools closed. On what basis? The evidence gathering can be sketchy in the extreme. The classroom inspection might only last ten minutes. There is only time for a tiny sample of exercise books to be checked. But every box in the checklist is completed and scored. The school is categorised and reports are written. Inspectors are not meant to help schools remedy their faults, as they do not wish to be held responsible for misleading advice.

But school inspectors can never simply observe and report. Their observations have unintended consequences, which can exacerbate an already difficult situation. There is always an uncertainty principle at work. At the now notorious Eydon Vale, Hanif Megat, the one inspector whose judgement I trusted and who had our best interests at heart, warned us of trouble ahead. To this day, no one had any idea what he meant, his words were so gnomic. Their effects were tragic, sowing discord among the Senior Managers, rippling through staff and pupils, dashing the hopes of an already precarious community.

What Megat told Sir Henry Robinson, the Chair of Trustees, was that Eydon Vale's leadership team reminded him of the crew of an airliner, which had taxied to the end of the runway. He thought that at the last minute, just as the plane was preparing for take-off, "One of you might be ejected from the cockpit."

Until that point, the re-inspection of Eydon Vale had gone surprisingly well. It was eight months after the school entered special measures that its Acting Head, Rhiannon Starr, received the phone call. The inspectors would be coming back just after the May half term. Their brief would be to judge how much progress Eydon Vale had made since it went into special measures and what the chances of its long-term viability would be. The previous judgement had put Eydon Vale in the worst sub-category of failing schools.

We had all been expecting news of the visit since mid-March. So, when Rhiannon informed us of the actual dates, our immediate response was relief. We were reasonably confident we had overcome the worst of our disciplinary problems. As the school's resident statistician reassured us, "The graph is still going down. The week we set it up, there had been 666 concerns about pupils' misbehaviour. It dropped to 330 by the start of the summer term. Last week it was standing at 191."

On their earlier visit, an HMI had been pelted with food in the lunch hall. This was also better policed. Previously, pupils had been allowed to jump the queue. Now, a surveillance camera had been placed above the checkout, while a lattice barrier ensured that only a single line of children could pass the serving hatches. Until that point, the kitchen staff had not realised how much pilfering had been taking place.

Pupil attendance rates crashed after Eydon Vale failed its inspection. They only went up again after the parents felt their children would be safe. It was now as good as ever, though still marginally below the floor set by Ofsted. In the previous inspection, several of the most disturbed and difficult pupils had been asked to absent themselves. This was no longer felt necessary.

Through her contacts in similar schools, Rhiannon gathered that the Inspectors would focus on discipline, teaching and pupil progress. So, the teachers were warned that they should followed our Guided Discipline Policy to the letter. They were also to have their six-week teaching plans ready to hand as HMI entered the classroom. All books were to be marked up to date over the half term. Positive examples of pupils' work were to be posted on classroom walls and corridors. With very few exceptions, the staff felt as well prepared as they could be.

A small group of Year 10 singers had taken part in a European choral festival earlier in the term. By the time the two HMI arrived, the foyer fielded a striking exhibition of their Italian posters and plaques. There were some gorgeous photographs taken by one of Eydon Vale's students of a Scuola Media by the Mediterranean. The room set aside for the HMI was hung with more photos and drawings of hard-working pupils by a talented Year 8.

The first day of the inspection was summery and bright. The Lead Inspector, Iona Salomon HMI, did not arrive until 9.15. Her colleague, Hanif Megat HMI, who had a fearsome reputation for closing failing schools, was delayed until 11.45. Their tardiness ensured that over the next two days, they could only have seen a maximum of 25 lessons. They also visited one assembly and two registration groups. No class was observed for over 30 minutes: most for less than a quarter of an hour.

Mrs Salomon seemed to have a specific agenda before she arrived. She had a clear hypothesis about the seriousness of the school's problems. The Inspectors would only see lessons in Science and ICT, English and Maths. Not only were these subjects seen as the core curriculum; they were the four departments most heavily criticised in the previous inspection.

Mrs Salomon wanted to interview the Acting Head, Miss Starr, after school on the first day, see the Chair of Trustees before school on the second day and meet a representative group of pupils on the final lunchtime. Megat would interview me as the Discipline and Standards Coordinator, meet a sample of parents and audit the pupils' exercise books.

It would be no exaggeration to say that both inspectors were startled by the effect of our discipline policy. All the pupils they questioned in classrooms and on the corridors knew the rules, rewards and sanctions by heart. The teachers insisted on eye contact. Pupils were putting up their hands rather than calling out in almost all the lessons. So, on the surface at least, there was a strong sense of order.

In one of the Year 10 Maths lessons taught by John Clayton, however, Hanif Megat observed more subtle signs of progress. It was based on the calculation of a percentage increase in the national minimum wage. As he entered the classroom, Megat noticed one of the girls resting her cheek on her hand as she looked towards the teacher. She seemed to be dreaming. However, after the teacher had finished telling the class how to tackle the questions, it was clear how hard she had been thinking about the Maths. She suggested an alternative and equally concise method. This example of reflection impressed him deeply. It was something he mentioned in his interview after school.

"There is no doubting your success in tackling inappropriate behaviour. Before I left my office, I was warned that I might be spattered with food or assaulted on the corridor, yet there are no such problems now. However, as I am sure you are aware, it is all too easy for managers in your position to curtail intellectual freedom in the name of good order. The kind of engagement with learning I observed in Mr Clayton's lesson is all too rare in the schools I'm asked to inspect.

"I see it as an indicator of the way that adolescents let themselves become absorbed in learning as soon as they feel safe. It normally seems to occur well after schools begin to stabilise. I generally pick it up in Arts and Humanities lessons first. But you have set the conditions for a talented Maths teacher like John Clayton to thrive. How did you do it?"

"As a young teacher, I had always wanted to develop a child-centred style," I explained. "But my initial experience in a chaotic Inner London comprehensive convinced me that this is easier said than done. It is only possible if pupils have a strong sense of boundaries. It is only where these are well established, that teachers can put children's curiosity at the heart of their teaching. Creating the conditions where curiosity thrives: that's the holy grail. In schools where the adults permit disorderly behaviour, learning of the quality you observed today becomes almost impossible."

"Would it be fair to describe your attitude to authority as nuanced?" the HMI suggested. He handed me a copy of the first talk I had given Eydon Vale staff on the restoration of order the previous

Christmas. Highlighted was the sentence: 'The sooner we implement these strategies, the sooner we get Ofsted off our backs.' "Where did you get this?" he asked.

"Miss Starr sent us all the paperwork she thought relevant to the inspection. I assumed she had checked it all with you first..."

"I believe that praise and reward are of most help in the learning process, not just with pupils, but also with teachers. In my view, Ofsted judgements are unnecessarily punitive. It might be more helpful if there were more specialist inspectors like you, who have turned around failing schools. Far too few know what it is like to stand in our shoes. The present Head of Ofsted is a banker with no teaching experience. People with your experience are all too rare."

Hanif shook his head warily. "Go on."

"Ofsted criteria have a spurious positivism. You make up the rules and do not allow alternative, ethical considerations. You make huge generalisations based on small samples. This can further disable children who have had a poor start in life. Eydon Vale has never had a good inspection report in the last 15 years. This has created a vicious cycle. None of your reports appears to have provided the insights needed for long-term progress. Many of the Inspectors who visit at-risk schools have only taught in advantaged areas. And the constant changes in your criteria create an aura of arbitrariness."

Few of the lessons that the Inspectors observed went as well as John Clayton's. At the end of the first day, the noise levels in a Year 8 small group discussion lesson soared just at the moment that the lead inspector entered an English class. A group of Year 10 pupils arrived late and unrepentant for ICT. A Maths lesson on triangular numbers with a less able group proved overambitious. The most serious incident that Mrs Salomon observed occurred in a supply teacher's lesson just before lunch on the second day.

The teacher had intended to show his Year 9 class a short film about the concept of the radioactive half-life, reinforce the main points with a PowerPoint and give them an experiment to carry out. Each table had a pack of 100 plastic coins. They were meant to toss them all individually, remove all those that had come up tails, tally up the heads and record the result on the graph, repeating the coin toss until none was left. The diminishing pile of coins was meant to represent the effects on the nucleus.

Iona Salomon, the Lead Inspector, entered the lab at the end of the PowerPoint introduction. Many of the pupils' heads were turned away from the teacher. Some were chattering quite brazenly. Few were listening to him. Hardly any appeared to have understood the connection between the practical experiment and the scientific theory. For many of the students, it was all a sort of game, whose rules they were going to subvert.

A boy in one corner waited until the teacher's back was turned and threw a handful of the plastic coins across the laboratory. A child in the opposite corner retaliated. As soon as he noticed what was happening, the member of staff phoned the Acting Head of Science. Hovering outside the door just in case of trouble, she had speedily removed the two troublemakers before anyone started throwing real coins across the classroom. No one was hurt, but the fragility of the teacher's authority had been exposed. Mrs Salomon was unamused.

Iona Salomon was a softly spoken, mild-mannered, Oxford-educated classicist. According to LinkedIn, her career path had taken her from an exclusive London private girls' college, where she quickly gained promotion, to the deputy headship of a grammar school. When her Headmaster had fallen ill, she was asked to act up. On his return to work, the Local Authority had offered her the post of Senior Adviser, with the proviso that she first trained as an Ofsted Inspector.

When Eydon Vale had first fallen into special measures, the Inspectors had said that the Trustees had failed to read the warning signs. So its chair, Sir Henry Robinson, had become much more personally involved than with most of the Trust's other schools. He had made space in his schedule to visit Eydon Vale twice a month and kept in regular telephone contact with both the Acting Head and me. In his interview with Mrs Salomon, Sir Henry had expressed his confidence that the crisis at Eydon Vale had passed. He was less concerned about HMI than the attitude of in one of the local papers, which appeared to have a vendetta against multi-academy trusts.

He gave the HMI a piercing, though not unfriendly, look as they filed into the Head's study for their final presentations to the Chair, the Acting Head and me. Iona Salomon took her time as she sorted through her papers. She spoke as if she was following a thoroughly rehearsed script, reducing her Oxford-accented judgements to pre-prepared official jargon. First, she thanked the school for its welcome, then commended the data and the package of school policies that Rhiannon Starr had put together.

"This was by far the most intelligent and objective guidance that I have ever had in any of the schools I have visited," she said, exchanging smiles with Miss Starr. "You grasped what we needed to know and where the strengths and weaknesses of the school lie. When Eydon Vale went into special measures, it was so unstable that HMI considered immediate closure. We accept your interpretation of the fall in the number of behavioural problems. Thanks to your disciplinary reforms, the school has now turned a corner. All our evidence suggests Eydon Vale is now stable.

"Ofsted judgements are often seen as unnecessarily negative," Iona Salomon smiled. "We are not allowed to use terms like 'Good' or 'Excellent' for failing schools, but in the opinion of my colleague, Mr Megat, the improvements in discipline and pastoral care are 'dramatic'. We did witness a few instances of misbehaviour, but they were quickly snuffed out before the trouble could spread. The corridors and lunch hall were also much quieter. Neither of us has ever seen such a rapid and profound turn around in any of the failing schools we have previously inspected.

"The parents and pupils that we have spoken to have also been very positive about all the changes you have introduced. They particularly appreciated your anti-bullying strategies, after-school classes and the improvements in special needs support. The haemorrhage in pupil numbers since the school went into special measures has been staunched, and the community has high hopes of the 'New Eydon'. We see no reason why you should not move into your new premises on schedule.

"In one-third of the lessons we observed the quality of teaching was 'good'. In 'good' lessons, we judged the pupils to be engaged in learning, rather than simply compliant. The teachers concerned had helped to extend pupils' thinking. Their work was challenging, and there were examples of effective support for pupils at all levels of ability. In the best lessons, there were examples of sophisticated discussions, involving two-thirds of the class. These enabled pupils to explore layers of meaning and derive alternative solutions to testing problems."

"Will that mean that Eydon Vale also comes out of special measures by the end of the term?" the Chair interrupted.

"Technically speaking, Eydon Vale will no longer exist after the end of this school year. Staff and pupils will be moving to new premises. The Secretary of State will probably turn to HMI for guidance, though, given the previous lack of oversight. Some 17 per cent of lessons we observed were still unsatisfactory. These were mainly taught by supply staff, most of whom may soon be leaving. So, a lot will depend on how good this year's GCSE results are and how well the new permanent staff settle in. However, you can almost certainly expect to see me again early in the new academic year."

As soon as the two HMI had left, Henry Robinson asked to see me privately. He congratulated me on the report. "It's a dizzying achievement. None of our other academies has come on so fast. If you had been here in November, Eydon Vale might never have been put in special measures. I need to pass on a warning from Hanif Megat, though. He thinks that just as the plane is ready for take-off, one of the crew might be ejected from the cockpit."

I was dumbfounded. What a strange message! "What on earth did he mean?" I asked Sir Henry. "We stand or fall as a team. Come what may, I have no intention of deserting this cockpit for at least five years, and I'm sure you feel the same. Was Megat playing mind games and trying to turn us against each other? Do you think he was advising us to move Rhiannon Starr on?"

The Chair of Trustees shook his head as if equally nonplussed. "I know you've had misgivings about her discipline. But she says you are a prima donna. And she says she doesn't always know whether you are playacting. Miss Starr is a pretty shrewd play-actor herself. She knows how to impress outsiders. She talks the Ofsted language. She's more diplomatic than you and can play their games. And you have to hand it to her: she is an excellent administrator. Mrs

Salomon could not have been more complimentary about her handling of the paperwork. I'd hate to see you two fall out.

"I'm relieved that you want to see the job through. There's no doubt you are the one to turn this ship around. You have prior experience. Your strategy is sound, and you have a feel for tactics. But if you were to apply elsewhere, I would not stand in your way."

Chapter Two: Prior Experience

Most people are embarrassed by failure. Talking about it breaks a taboo. But I have been compelled to keep describing how I came to be at Eydon Vale and what I witnessed there. So, I have retold my story, first as a journal, then as a blog, now as a novella. As time passed, I have had to ask myself what drew me to this aspect of education. What was my own prior experience of failure?

Just before my fifth birthday, my parents took me for an interview at a "good" infants school a mile away from our house. My vocabulary must have impressed the Headteacher, for she predicted that I would go to Cambridge one day. I enjoyed school, especially the "Music and Movement" lessons in the Hall. It was a new building and the free school dinners were almost as good as my mother's. Every night, when my father asked me about school, I told him I had been awarded a gold star.

The fact was that my first term was a disaster, however. I could not draw anything recognisable and by the first Parents' Evening had made no start on reading or writing. The reception teacher, Mrs Mason, was extremely blunt. She told my father that I must be either deaf, blind or stupid. The humiliation was terrible. I was unmasked as both a retarded reader and a liar.

The problem was quickly remedied. At the shop on the High Street, I stared out at a couple of passing red London buses, as the optician explained to my mother that I was so long-sighted that I was seeing double. Does not everyone see two buses, I wondered. The optician referred me to a wheezing consultant ophthalmologist, and as he peered into my eyeballs, he warned my mother that I might go blind by the time I was 50. With my new glasses, I could now understand the squiggles on the page. I quickly caught up the rest of the class. I realised that I could read silently inside my head before Mrs Mason showed the rest of the class how to do it. I hated the storybooks we had to work through, though. The illustrated readers about rabbits and farm animals in dog-eared cardboard covers were imbued with all the humiliation of my initial failure.

My new interest was in history. That was what I preferred to read. History was real. The day we first learned about the Vikings, I was ecstatic. I raced out into the playground as the lone warrior, overcoming all resistance in my imaginary horned hat. That none of the other children wanted to join my game of Monks and Vikings dumbfounded me.

My father was all too happy to encourage my new love of learning. Just before we sat the 11+, I read a book about the history of science. It established my lifelong suspicion that knowledge was neither static nor confined to what teachers told you. Science had its own Viking warriors, who went ahead of the rest, challenging dogma and the authorities. It thrived on free expression and underwent revolutions.

No doubt, for the lucky few, Dulwich College provided an outstanding secondary education. For Latin and Greek, we had Philip Vellacott, Penguin Books' translator of the Oedipus plays. He made sense of grammar for us and encouraged us to write Latin verse. Laurie Jagger taught us how to construct a balanced and objective argument. Raymond Wilson. He was a published poet, compiler of children's anthologies and contributor to Radio 3. He taught our group in Year 11, just before he left school teaching to become a professor of education. He was quite clear that Year 11 should be a voyage of personal discovery. We had to write a mini-dissertation on a poet of our choice, to be examined through a university-style viva in front of the class. We would have to study the "O" level set texts in our own time.

Ever since my late start in reading, I had always found English the most difficult and unappealing of subjects, but this could hardly have been a better age to discover poetry. Like my friend Graham Swift, I spent hours after homework writing my own stories.

Just before the "O" level English exam, I had a nightmarish awakening. I realised that my sentence structures lacked rigour and rhythm. I would write a line or two, scrunch up the paper, throw it in the bin and start again. In my attempt to reconstruct my style, I lost the knack of essay writing that Laurie Jagger had so patiently taught us all. Within weeks, everything started to fall apart. It was as if my unease about language began to corrupt my knowledge bank, just like a virus annihilating a computer memory. My "A" levels were a disaster and I fell into an adolescent depression, which only lifted in my final Oxbridge Scholarship term.

All through our "A" levels, the Head of History had been giving us one lesson a week on the history of ideas. I devoured Nietzsche. "Facts are precisely what they are not: only interpretations" might not be good philosophy. Yet it summed up the quagmire my history essays had fallen into. Nietzsche made the utterance of truth a prime virtue. His embattled rage seemed to epitomise the one thing I had learned from my teenage angst: "Truth has to be fought for every step of the way". If I could not say what I meant and mean what I said, I would be locked away inside my solipsistic hell for the rest of my life.

Towards the end of Year 13, I asked if I could present a paper on the philosophy of education. I knocked on David Lindsay's door and asked for his help. He was the neighbour who had tutored me for the 11+ exam. He introduced me to the libertarian ideals of Rousseau and Maria Montessori. I visited the Primary School, where he was the Headteacher and saw his school's child-centred learning for myself.

Like Raymond Wilson at Dulwich, David Lindsay believed that children should base their study of literature on creative writing. Unlike Wilson, Lindsay's successes were not limited to the few. His was an inclusive school: most pupils came from the local council estate; the rest were travellers and Roma. Many of them had made a slow start in reading, just like me. The poetry they had written had grown out of their everyday experience, some of which was bleak. And yet it was boldly displayed in all the classrooms and corridors, alongside the children's artwork.

Revolution was in the air in my last term at Dulwich. Someone had daubed the anti-apartheid symbol on the College clock tower. There were sit down strikes protesting against the prefects' power to cane younger boys. I edited the final old-style official school magazine and ensured there was a special insert celebrating the poetry of Ian Macdonald. He and I had set up a scurrilous anti-school poetry magazine and run a poetry club.

The drama I directed won the school cup for an excoriating interpretation of *The Insect Play* transposed to 1960s Dulwich. The young Peter Bazalgette, who became the Head of the Arts Council, was an astonishing tramp. He fell off the stage at his entrance and smashed his prop liquor bottle in the stalls.

Every week, all those applying to Oxbridge for English would meet at Ian Macdonald's house to read the Shakespeare plays that were not on the "A" level syllabus. For the first time, I began to think for myself about Shakespearian poetry and drama. I forged a new essay technique just in time for the Scholarship papers. These were deemed good enough for a place at Caius.

Jeremy Prynne, the hermetic poet and our Director of Studies, told us that we would learn as much from our late-night conversations with each other as from any formal study. He and Paul Wheeler stood out as by far the most talented people I had ever met: indeed, the equal of any genius I had ever read about. In all of that term, Paul never seemed to use the same word twice: the songs he had written were both beautiful and true; his fondness for friends and of his suburban family a philosophical statement. His girlfriend was John Lennon's secretary and he jammed with the Beatles.

I introduced Paul to my Dulwich friends, like Ian Macdonald and Graham Swift. He introduced me to Robert Kirby and Nick Drake. One lunchtime, as he and a group of friends sat in the Caius' bar, talk turned to the fairly recently discovered mechanisms through which DNA reproduced itself. To my amazement, no one else seemed to understand DNA's function as an information processing system or the reproduction of life as patterns of instructions. So as a kind of joke, I quickly unzipped and zipped up my fly, demonstrating the way RNA encoded the chemicals that were needed in exactly the right order. Everybody else laughed, but Paul looked me in the eye and told me I had just got to be a teacher.

I was chagrined. I wanted to become a writer, a novelist, a poet. But the more I thought about it, the more discriminating his judgement appeared. A career in schools had never been my aim. After all that had happened in my final years at Dulwich, it was quite likely I would never feel entirely comfortable in classrooms. But if I did have a special talent for teaching, then maybe the profession chose me.

Jeremy Prynne had been quite seriously ill with jaundice when we went up and he had been unable to supervise all 14 in our group. Half were farmed out to other fellows. By the end of our second year, it was clear that several of us were in trouble. Between the end of the exams and results day, Prynne invited a group of us out to lunch in a Greek café. Round the table were seated some of his most talented students, including Paul Wheeler. Andrew Cunningham, who later created *Badger and Bodger* for children's TV was there, as was the musicologist, Pete O'Connor, who later became a university teacher in Japan. I got a 2:1. All the others were sent down.

Paul was shattered. He had been in the university the day the results were published but had been unable to find his name anywhere on the lists. When you failed your exams in Cambridge, you became a non-person. He drove across the outskirts of London with his girlfriend Diana to ask me what on earth he should do. The fact that his dissertation on Jane Austen had been awarded 96% counted for nothing. He had written iconoclastic answers on a couple of papers and been made a scapegoat. Exams were a charade and Paul had been judged expendable. I had assumed that failure was a personal affair. I had not realised how systemic it was in education. I did not know what to say to him.

Educational failure went well beyond my private anguish: beyond the experience of losing the ability to write "A" level essays: beyond even the wastage of talents like Paul's in degree courses. As I discovered in my final year at Cambridge, the UK had one of the longest tails of underachievement in the developed world. In those days, only Grammar School pupils and the top streams of the secondary moderns were entered for "O" levels. The great majority of British children left school without any qualifications. At least 2% of our school leavers were completely illiterate; 10% would have lifelong problems with reading.

It became clear to me that the poor skills of underprivileged school leavers were not only a scandal: they would act as a life-long brake on the productivity of our whole economy. The government would only tolerate such massive and endemic failure so long as the relative wealth and privileges of their higher social classes were maintained. According to some of the sociologists I read before and during my initial teacher training course, not only was the examination system rigged: even working-class language was penalised.

In those days, all the Secondary School PGCE students were expected to observe teaching in a local primary school before the course started. So, I spent a fortnight at a white, middle class, Church School near our flat. It was quite different from David Lindsay's school. There was no attempt to fashion a child-centred curriculum. The Year 6 classroom to which I was sent was laid out in rows and columns. The male teacher, who was obviously regarded by his Headteacher as a paragon, taught from the chalkboard at the front of the class. The clever children sat nearest him. I was told to sit with two non-readers at the back.

Neither of these girls had a clue what was going on in that class. The teacher could have been speaking Ancient Greek for all the sense he made to them. Even when I read aloud to them from the textbooks that they had been given, they barely understood. The vocabulary was far too difficult for them and they were too embarrassed to listen to me. They could barely add or subtract.

The tutor that Goldsmiths' had allotted me was Margot Heinemann. I recognised her name from the dedication of a poem in the Penguin Book of 30s poetry. She had been the darling of left-wing intellectuals, joining the Communist Party whilst at Cambridge. She had researched the nationalisation of the coal industry for the Labour Party. She told me that her first taste of teaching came at the Cadbury's Continuation School where she was given a class of 14-year-olds on day release from the chocolate factory.

Our initial appointment was a meeting of minds. When I indicated my interest in how children fail, she asked me if I would like to do a course on remedial reading. This was to be held in a boys' secondary modern school called Sir Philip Magnus in the red-light district behind Kings Cross. Gradually, as the week drew on, the complexities of the reading process were made clear to us.

An advisory teacher called John Wallbridge explained all the latest theories he had picked up in the Remedial Education Centre at Birmingham University. We covered the use and limitations of the various reading tests: difficulties with letter/ sound correspondences: phonemes, digraphs and syllabification: sight vocabulary and context cues: literal and inferential comprehension: readability and reading schemes. There was a chance to analyse children's artwork in terms of Freudian dynamics. Every so often, we could hear gangs of boys thundering down the corridors and banging on our door. The rest of the school was in chaos, but John Wallbridge seemed to know what he was doing.

For my top set Year 9s, I was determined to organise a programme of study based on the reading and writing of poetry. This was quite an alien concept and the lads made hardly any effort in our first lesson, working through my initial worksheet half-heartedly and barely attempting the final task, which required them to write a poem. At the start of my second lesson, I lined up the class against the corridor wall and made it clear that I expected much more effort and better behaviour from them.

After I had marched them inside, I read them the first poem Seamus Heaney ever wrote: "Digging". I told them he was from a large farming family on the border between Eire and Northern Ireland, where the threat of guns was never far away. I recounted the story of how he started writing. The poem had come to him as he was driving back home through narrow country lanes, changing gears as he turned a sharp corner.

I told them about the turning point in my own education, when Raymond Wilson had taught us that there is no higher calling than writing poetry. I promised that if only they could take a leap off the cliff and write their own work in their own language, this would transform their experience of life and school. Any decent efforts would be printed out and displayed on the classroom walls.

And it worked. They sat silently over their worksheets. In the initial comprehension questions, they picked out the references to the pen resting in Seamus' hand, "snug as a gun". Many of the children in front of me were recent immigrants from poor agricultural communities in Europe and the Caribbean. They could put themselves in Heaney's place and understood how profoundly the life of countrymen in his community had been changing.

In mimicking the precision of Heaney's imagery, they began producing poems of their own that came from somewhere deep inside. The very next lesson I taught that class, Margot Heinemann dropped in. The poems that they had just written were on display on the classroom walls. The boys were still on their best behaviour. She confirmed me in the feeling that I had made the right choice of career.

My first posting was at Tulse Hill Secondary Modern Boys' School in Brixton. It was a wild and unpredictable place. Some of the games that the boys played were very rough. The school was housed in a single cuboid, like a giant matchbox on its side, and it was eight storeys tall. One class with a lesson on the top floor smuggled whole bricks from the building site into a lesson. Every time the teacher turned to the chalkboard, these would be lobbed out of the windows onto the staff car park below. Windscreens were broken and car bonnets badly dented. They had caused hundreds of pounds of damage.

As my Year 9 class lined up for another teacher's lesson, one of my pupils attacked a boy with pointed scissors. I had had no training in containing violence and reacted unthinkingly, pulling the aggressor away. As he lashed out at me, I warded the scissors away with my forearm. He broke the skin on the back of my hand and drew blood. Other teachers took the assailant away and he was suspended from school for a week. But at least the Year 9s realised I would not tolerate violence. A boundary was drawn. No one ever hit me again throughout my teaching career.

Apart from my Year 9 English class, I also had a Year 9 History class, a Year 7 Integrated Humanities class and remedial reading. Fresh from my evening classes with John Wallbridge, I arrogantly informed the Head of History, Carolyn Griffin, that the readability level of the school textbook was far too high for the bulk of my Year 9 class. Some of the children were illiterate and many others were semi-literate. I asked her if I could use the topics we were meant to cover for the end of year exams as the basis for a more interactive approach, which intermingled the Anglocentric and African perspectives. I promised Carolyn I would write a new episode of this semi-improvised historical novel each week, which would be cyclostyled and read around the class. And she very generously agreed.

About a third of the intake at Tulse Hill had reading ages of eight or less. All probationary teachers like me were encouraged to spend half a dozen lessons a week in the remedial department, team teaching them. Most of the time, this meant hearing them read from a selection of the easy reading novellas about white, English teenagers John Wallbridge had shown us.

This approach was quite different from what I had been taught by John Wallbridge. If the children were good at sight recognition, they thrived on the attention. But most of them had serious flaws in their knowledge of phonics and there was no attempt to analyse or remedy these. The one great advantage of Tulse Hill's scheme was it broke down the barriers between young teachers and reluctant learners. We would sit on the comfortable chairs, patiently reading a simplified text together, where every phrase was set out on a new line and there were pictures on every page. This enabled us to listen to the children and learn to empathise with them. And at the end of the year, when I became the Head of Remedial in a Midlands Comprehensive, I put the fusion of these two strategies at the heart of my work.

My new Head, Gordon Rees, gave me every encouragement to further my skills in Special Needs Education. All he asked was that I write termly reports about the progress of the poor readers and keep him abreast of my ideas. On our first summer holiday in Daventry, I spent a fortnight helping out at an approved school, learning all about behaviour modification and positive reinforcement. During the next, Rees paid for a course at the Marriage Guidance Centre in Rugby and let me provide counselling for one or two of the most distressed children during lesson time. One Summer Term, when my "O" level group had left, I was even allowed to spend one day a week teaching in a nearby day special school for "maladjusted" children.

Ever since I had started teaching, I had been searching for a disciplinary approach that combined clear boundaries with intellectual freedom. The clue that I had looking for came from an old book about client-centred counselling by Carl Rogers that I picked up on the counselling course in Rugby. In his chapter on student-centred teaching, Rogers asked:

If instead of focusing all our interest on the teacher – What shall I teach? How can I prove I have taught it? How can I cover all that I should teach? – we focused our interest on the student, the questions and the issues would all be different.

Rogers was turning all the accepted views of education upside down. He argued that teacher listening might have more potential than the conventional combination of "chalk and talk" and teacher's questions. That chapter led me into completely new speculations about my teaching. What if I refused to teach a class? What if I stopped asking pupils questions? What if we just read a long poem together, stopping every few verses, for them to ask me questions?

I wanted to start the experiment with a new and lively Year 9 mixed ability class. That term's set text was Coleridge's *The Ancient Mariner*. I warned them that this was an exceptionally difficult poem. Even with the annotations that Coleridge had left, university lecturers were still finding it difficult to grasp what he had meant. We would read a couple of verses. Then anyone in the class could feel free to ask me a question. If they caught me out and I honestly did not know the answer, I would give them a prize as positive reinforcement.

At first, the children were uncertain of what I wanted. They suspected my motives. The first questions they asked were like a parody of typical teacher questions. "What is the first word on line 9 of page 13?" Then, some of the more successful students came out with more pertinent but still closed questions. It was a puzzle. They knew from experience that most teachers try to avoid questions to which they do not know the answers.

Eventually, as it became clear that I had no objections to these, the class began to grasp a little of the academic pursuit. At last, one plucked up the courage to ask a question about something she had not understood. When I gave her positive feedback, a few others joined in. After about a fortnight's lessons, I had to admit that I did not know the answer to one of the children's questions and that I suspected no one else did either.

At that point, I changed the rules again. Not only would I refuse to teach the class, but I would also refuse to answer their questions. I would simply act as a moderator, maintaining good order and positively reinforcing good thinking. But all the pupils' questions would be referred back to the class. This further whetted the children's appetite for knowledge and understanding.

By this time, we had reached the climax of the poem, when the trails of the sea creatures are transformed into phosphorescence. The most able and original boy in the class simply asked, "What on earth does this poem mean?" There was a pause in which the rest simply contemplated their intellectual limitations. At this point, Tony, the boy in the class with the lowest reading age and the worst criminal record, put his hand up and answered, "This poem is about beauty!"

Over the five years I taught at that Midlands Comprehensive, virtually all the English teachers joined the rotating, remedial support group. But there were also PE, Maths and History teachers and Heads of Year, who taught children to read. HMI heard about what we were doing, and a team came to investigate. This was well before the advent of Ofsted. In those days, the inspectors were curious and open-minded. The three things that most interested them were the withdrawal of children from mixed-ability classes by a circus of subject teachers; the entry of my top set for "O" level English one year early and the decline in the numbers of our pupils attending juvenile court. But the question I wanted them to answer was what proportion of teachers needed the experience of such programmes before less able children began to feel a sense of belonging to the school. And, of course, they had no answer to that.

They might not have answered my questions, but they did include an account of the way a range of Southbrook teachers were taught how to analyse and remedy reading deficits in an HMI booklet. After six years of teaching, I now had a clear idea of the reasons why individual pupils failed to read. What I had yet to consider was how the English Education system could tolerate educational failure on such a scale. So, I asked the head if I could take a Master's in Special Education at Birmingham University.

The course was a disappointment. Few of the lectures were interesting or original. The lecturers seemed to prefer critiquing others' research, much of it out of date. Week after week, Professor Ron Gulliford would bring in old research papers for our special education seminar group to discuss. It was fun seeking out the flaws in their evidence or methodology, but the standards in the study of education did seem appallingly low.

Gulliford introduced us to the work of J E Collins, a psychologist whom he had known at Birmingham University, questioning the long-term effectiveness of remedial reading. It was an even older article, dating from 1948. Colins wanted to differentiate between "backward" children, who had low IQs, and "retarded readers" with average or high IQs, who had what we would now call specific learning difficulties or dyslexia.

Collins had quite rightly assumed that if he paid close attention to the deficits in the reading skills of the "retarded readers" and devised drills to overcome them, they would quickly catch up. He divided his small group of "retarded readers" into control and experimental groups. The experimental groups made rapid short-term gains.

However, when Collins had followed up the children "retarded readers" group over the following years, he found that their progress stalled. After three years, the control group had caught them up. It was an unusually brilliant paper and all subsequent research in this area confirmed Collins' depressing findings. I sensed that he lacked a sociological understanding, though. Collins had assumed that the only important variable was the remedial reading programme. He had not taken whole-school or societal context into account.

Even after the bout of intensive remedial reading tuition had been completed, Southbrook's poor readers continued to make progress, though. Their reading had been tested when they joined the school, at six-monthly intervals while they were having the tuition and annually until they left school. I had well over a hundred test results going back over five years that confirmed this.

Sure enough, the progress of the poor readers had slowed after the bout of intensive remedial tuition had been completed. But it did not level out, as Collins would have predicted. So why was this? It took me the whole of my year in Birmingham to solve this puzzle. My conclusion was that by involving a circus of sympathetic staff in experientially based reading interventions, we had begun to change the ecology of the school. This finding became the cornerstone of the book I published the next year.

During my year at Birmingham, Ian Sinclair and Ed Vulliamy, two sociologists from York, wrote an article in *The Times Educational Supplement* savaging the lack of a sociological perspective in the Warnock Report. They called it "one-sided" and "blinkered". They argued that it failed to examine "the structural and attitudinal constraints that prevent the educational system from serving equally well all groups in society."

I dashed off a riposte, inviting all those interested in carving out a new sociology of special education to join me for a colloquium at Birmingham University. I did not book a room. We all just arrived at the doors of the Education Department, found the rotunda unlocked and introduced ourselves. Those who attended included Len Barton, who subsequently became Dean of the Institute of Education in London; and Sally Tomlinson, who later held chairs at Lancaster University, the University of Wales and Goldsmiths.

It was probably the most hilarious and productive meeting I ever chaired. The time was ripe for a completely new paradigm: the "social model of disability". At that guerrilla meeting, Len Barton offered to set up the journal *Disability and Society*. This was later given the accolade of the "world's leading journal in disability studies". I now felt ready to take up a post as a Temporary Lecturer in Special Education at Durham University.

The spark for my first book came from a talk given to our students by Lambert Bignell, a humane and approachable HMI. His theme was that all children should be led by their curiosity and dignified by their learning. Few of the students in that group were based in primary schools, and Bignell developed his theory that the lack of Maths or English *Departments* in primary schools enabled teachers to follow the children's interests more readily across curriculum boundaries. Their subject leaders were called *coordinators*. The idea came to me: why not do away with remedial education? Why not have Special Needs Coordinators in every school?

At that time, most of the children with special needs were either left to sink or swim in mixed ability classes or hived off into special schools or bottom streams. These groups would be designated "remedial" or "progress" classes. What I wanted was nothing less than the transformation of current practice, a means of raising low expectations and ensuring that these children had a more stimulating and appropriate education. The low-status Heads of Remedial, who had been unwittingly colluding with these poor expectations, would be replaced with "Special Needs Coordinators" or SENCos, whose main responsibility was to act as school-based agents of change.

The children with special needs and their learning deficits had been the main focus of the old Heads of Remedial. The SENCo's first and overriding responsibility would be with the teachers. S/he would enable staff from across the curriculum to reach out "forcefully and successfully" to these children. The SENCos would initially train a select group of these teachers to teach small sets of underachieving children the 3Rs. The SENCos' second responsibility would be to get these teachers to challenge existing practices in their curricular areas, through a greater understanding of the roles of oracy, literacy and numeracy. And thirdly, the SENCos would enable mainstream schools to integrate the children with physical, sensory, cognitive and behavioural difficulties, who would soon be leaving special schools as the Warnock Report became accepted.

When my temporary post as a University Lecturer ended, I was sure my ideas about Special Needs Coordinators would be forgotten. But, much to my disbelief, they caught on. Interviewed in Bradford for an Adviser's job, I was told that every school in the Education Authority had a SENCo. One evening after school, I had a telephone call from Montréal, asking me if I would like to tell the week-long AQETA conference, "the largest convention of special ed. teachers in North America" about SENCos. Even the Education Department in Cambridge invited me to run a summer school.

When the school's adviser found out, he suggested I apply for the post of Senior Teacher in charge of the newly created Special Unit for children with physical disabilities at Rectory Road School. Almost immediately, I was promoted to Deputy Head. This purpose-built, inclusive comprehensive in a drug-riddled, decaying, council estate on the edges of a post-industrial wasteland was the ideal preparation for Eydon Vale.

It took most of that Summer Term to get to know the children who would be joining us from the special school. Ever since Tulse Hill, I had been visiting parents in their own homes as a means of understanding the children's capabilities. I was simply astonished at what these disabled children could do outside school. Neville lived and worked on the family farm. Confined to an electric wheelchair all day at the special school, he could climb the farmhouse stairs unaided. During my visit, he crawled over to the tractor, drove it around the yard and manoeuvred its front loader bucket.

Certainly, in the short term, we would need a couple of classes in the unit for the physically disabled children who could not read simple monosyllabic words or count past five. However, it would have been far too easy for these to become a new special school within Rectory Road. We had to find a way of training the mainstream staff to teach them in the unit. We needed a way of training inexperienced mainstream teachers how to work with children with special needs. The staff from the special school would "flow out" of the unit to spend a few lessons in the mainstream and in return a select group of mainstream teachers would "flow into" the unit to teach PE, Science, Modern Foreign Languages, History, Geography, RE and Sex Education.

Death had never been mentioned at the special school, even though it occurred so regularly. There was a disproportionally large number of families with the Duchenne Muscular Dystrophy gene in the area. In those days, life expectancy only extended until the late teens. Some of our children lost their ability to walk at 11, to write independently at 15. These boys could not think of anything other than impending death. In such a context, what was the purpose of education? How should we deal with the anger that made them drive their electric wheelchairs hard at the teaching assistants and pin them to the walls?

Education could function as a distraction from painful realities. Creative art and music; smells and bangs in chemistry; hectic wheelchair basketball in the gym; shared readings of affecting novels: only these could briefly keep the demons at bay. The homeless, suicidal and troubled mainstream children, who came under our wing in the special unit, also helped create a kind of solidarity. Those with a limited life expectancy were not alone. Life may have been a mean business, but at least there could be camaraderie among the distressed.

One sunny Friday morning, not long after we moved into the unit, one of the boys with a chronic degenerative condition died. Under the old regime, this would never have been publicly acknowledged. This time, all the parents were contacted. We would hold a brief assembly after lunch to announce his death and allow all the children in the unit to remember the boy's life. The parents would be welcome to join us. We expected that most of the children would want to stay in school after the assembly and spend the rest of the afternoon chatting quietly, but they could take them home early if they preferred.

In the event, what we staged was a kind of *Death Café*. Small groups of chairs were laid out and cups of tea distributed. The children were able to air all kinds of questions, comments and feelings with the staff and each other. Several cried and had to be comforted. And it gave some of the older children, who had resented the closure of the special school, an opportunity to vent their anger and sense of powerlessness.

From then on, there was hardly a year when a child did not die. The parents grew to recognise the role the school had assumed and would ask the undertakers to drive the cortege through the school car park on the child's final journey. Lessons would be suspended and nearly all of the 600 Rectory Road pupils would stand silently as it passed.

Not all the children who died had disabilities. About two-thirds of the able-bodied pupils came from the Rectory Estate. Originally built to service post-war primary industries, in chemicals, the railways and shipyards, it had suffered terribly under Margaret Thatcher. Deindustrialisation meant that every year, whole families were made redundant. Suicides, teenage pregnancies and delinquency rates rose sharply.

The behaviour of some of these mainstream pupils was such a problem we had to rethink our pastoral care. Guided Discipline was based on the principles of behaviour modification I had first encountered in my summer holiday job at the approved school. Central to the system was the menu of rewards. These had to be agreed with the pupils. Similarly, the menu of sanctions had to be agreed with the staff. The rules had to unambiguous and easily remembered. There needed to be fast, comprehensive and transparent data collection for rule infringement. My only criticism of existing training packages such as Lee Canter's Assertive Discipline was that a few lectures at the start of the term were insufficient. Senior Managers had to visit every teacher twice a week to provide ongoing reinforcement and guidance.

Assertive Discipline would never have worked with our bullies, either. The estate that Rectory Road Comprehensive served was nicknamed "cocaine city". Our children would only dare inform on bullies if we could guarantee anonymity. One of the Year 10s who dared to tell us about one of his friend's problems came to school the next day with terrible bruises on his face. He said he'd got too close to a man practising his golf swing on the school field. Six months later he had a brain haemorrhage. His powers of speech never recovered. So, we invented "secret friends" to circumvent the power of the drug enforcers.

We also found that voluntary extra classes for able and talented pupils did not work. Our after school, Saturday morning and vacation classes had to be compulsory if we were to transform our exam results. Two years before I joined Eydon Vale, I had written an article for *Disability and Society* summarising what we had done to ensure that Rectory Road not only felt safe: its value-added scores were in the top 1% for English schools. This became the basis of the Action Plan for Eydon Vale.

Chapter Three: On the Threshold

OFSTED is a constant pressure on failing schools like Eydon Vale. Some Academy Trusts buy into this. They pick Heads who will bully the staff. The Heads expect the teachers to bully the kids. The awkward ones are mown down, like a lawnmower flattening the grass. Children who break the rules are penned up in punishment carrels, sent home or taken off roll. Exam results often improve, especially in the short term, but as I had learned on my Master's course, long term trends are more significant.

Eydon Vale had just failed its Ofsted when the post of deputy head was advertised. John Silver, Rectory Road's Head – and incidentally the most effective headteacher I ever worked with – showed me the advert. I telephoned Rhiannon Starr, Eydon Vale's new Acting Head, and was offered a visit and a chance to see the plans for the new school building.

From the car park, it sounded as if all its 700 children must have been shouting at once. As I waited in Reception for Miss Starr to show me around, the bell rang for lunch. To reach her study, we had to pass the hall. There was no queue. Older, bigger children simply pushed their way to the front. As I looked inside, one of the table-tops had become unlatched. All the food and drink slid into the children's laps.

Rhiannon was slight but vibrant. Her gentle North Welsh accent belied her fierce ambition. A couple of years previously she had applied to be the second deputy at Rectory Road. Almost 20 years my junior, she had had no previous experience of tough schools, but I liked her then and sensed an opportunity for real partnership now. She nodded at the dining hall and explained, "It's their idea of a joke. It's bullying, of course, and it's completely out of hand. One of the Inspectors had food thrown over his suit."

"And those struts on the walls?" I asked her, pointing at the metal braces that lined the corridors.

"They originally held CCTV cameras to monitor vandalism and internal truancy," the Acting Head replied. "They did not last long, though. They were all stolen within the month."

At that moment, a mob thundered past us. Rhiannon stood aside, but one lad clipped my shoulder. "The inspectors said the movement around the school was chaotic. One of them put his arms out to stop a kid tearing around the corridors during lessons, but he charged him down. He called him 'frit' to his face."

Not since my time at Tulse Hill School had I experienced such disorder. But Eydon Vale's students were more oppositional, more mutinous. "Why aren't such boys expelled?" I asked her.

"Oh, they were. The Head suspended 160 in his last half term. Just before he was fired, he permanently excluded two dozen Year 9s, but the boy who knocked into you was a Year 9, who wasn't bad enough for the cull."

The speed with which the interviews were arranged was impressive. It appeared that Eydon Vale had been put "in serious weaknesses", the category just above failure, in the previous April. There were no forms to fill in. Miss Starr just needed a curriculum vitae and a letter of application. As I was later informed, the Headteacher and the Chair of the Governing Body had been "let go" just the week before the vacancy was advertised. They and the LEA had negotiated a confidentiality clause in the agreement, so precisely how the school had got into such difficulties always remained opaque.

There were few clues on the internet. April's Ofsted Report even commended the previous Headteacher's planning for a move to new school buildings. As it pointed out, Eydon Vale did serve one of Holmesside's poorer areas, although its deprivation scores were not as severe as Rectory Road's. It did have one of the largest populations of traveller children in the UK. Roma children have arguably the lowest educational attainments of any ethnic group in Europe, though this had never been a problem for David Lindsay.

Interviews took place when the school was closed for half term. Without the children, Eydon Vale had an even more desolate air. There were three interviewing panels in the morning. My first was composed of the oldest pupils. I asked them if they had had their time again, would they have chosen to attend Eydon Vale School. Faced with such a question, most teenagers would probably have been ambivalent. It is "uncool" to admit too much loyalty to one's secondary school.

However, these Year 11 pupils were beyond despair. They could not name one thing they liked about Eydon Vale. A girl called Gillian Newsome said that what worried her most was that, four terms into her GCSE programme, she had not even had a practice English exam essay.

And she wanted to know what I would do about the bullying. So, I explained how "secret friends" worked.

The afternoon's panel for the three shortlisted candidates included three Parent Governors, Rhiannon and the Chair of Trustees, Sir Henry Robinson. His multi-academy trust had just been invited to take over the failing Eydon Vale. At six feet seven inches tall, he struck an imposing figure with a full beard and piercing, black eyes. According to his entry in LinkedIn, Sir Henry had had a brief stint as a teacher in outer London. Family pressures had led to a spell in charge of his father's ailing furniture shop. Having created a successful chain of retail outlets, he had sold the business and returned to education at the head of the Robinson Family Trust. Its reputation for boosting exam results, confronting underperforming teachers and "lawnmowing" troublesome pupils had led to its rapid expansion. His questions were far more incisive than anyone else's. The way that he weighed his words established a clear vision of the qualities of leadership needed for such a school.

Sir Henry's first question was about the care of the new building. "The repair bill for broken windows at Eydon Vale has been running at nearly £20 000 per term. Damage to classroom furniture added another £10 000. What would you do to prevent such vandalism here?"

"If I were appointed, I would zone the New Eydon," I replied. "I would have distinctive colour schemes and carpeting for each, with heavy fire doors demarcating the boundaries. So far as Eydon Vale is concerned, most of the vandalism appears to be the work of internal truants. Zoning would break the school down into much more manageable spaces. Each zone would be the responsibility of a Head of Faculty, assisted by a Head of Year and a Head of House.

"They would oversee behaviour in classrooms and corridors. The pupils will have to be taught how to move around the building properly, look after the toilets and make better use of the lunch hall. After all the chaos of the past few years, I would not even allow the pupils off the premises at lunchtime."

"And this would be your priority?" asked Miss Starr.

"No, no, no! Pupil discipline is the first issue we have to crack. Few schools are as disorderly as Eydon Vale. To create a more successful learning environment, we would need to change the existing norms and set clear boundaries. New rules and sanctions have a part to play, but by themselves, they wouldn't be enough. Eydon Vale needs a new Disciplinary Policy, based on praise and reward, which wins the trust of the majority of students.

"All my career, I've been looking for ways of rebuilding trust. I think I've found it in an approach called 'Guided Discipline'. If I were appointed, I would ask the trustees for permission to close the school on the last day of this term and teach the staff its principles. I would ask the Trust to set aside a training budget so that every teacher could be issued with a Guided Discipline manual to read over the Christmas holidays. I would also like the school closed on the first day after New Year. All teachers, administrative assistants, support staff and trustees would then be invited to agree on the new rules, rewards and sanctions."

"And you think praise and rewards would be sufficient to alter the way these children behave?" asked Sir Henry.

"Guided Discipline has a proven record of success in some of the most violent, drug-ridden and disadvantaged areas of the United States. I implemented it at Rectory Road. What I found, though, was that simple lectures go in one ear and out the other. Reading the manual is slightly more productive. Even the workshops I'm proposing would barely scratch the surface. Telling staff is not enough. I would need to visit every classroom in the school at least twice a week to see for myself how well each of the teachers was putting it into practice.

"We don't have the expertise within the academy chain to embark on such a training programme," said the Chair of Trustees.

"I'm part of the UK training group, so it would not cost the Trust a penny."

"What upsets my children," said Alice Lawton's mother as Parent Trustee, "is the abuse on social media." Alice would turn out to be in my Year 11, top set English class.

"That's a desperately tricky problem, I agree. A lot of Heads feel out of their depth with social media. Rumours spread quickly and in schools as unsettled as Eydon Vale, the children lose all trust in the powers-that-be to get things under control. What I found is that if we put a stop to the physical bullying and make the pupils feel they don't have to worry about getting hurt, it's much easier to stop verbal and online abuse."

"We've got some seriously disturbed children here, dumped on us by our competitors..." added Mrs Lawton.

"Yes, I'd heard similar stories from the pupils who interviewed me this morning. In an educational marketplace, it suits all the other schools to have a sink school with surplus places, where they can off-roll their most disruptive pupils. They add to the existing problems of schools like Eydon Vale. It strikes me we have to distinguish between the misbehaviour of the great number of ordinary pupils, which has only come about because of the collapse in discipline, and the management of the few with psychological difficulties. We can only address the needs of these individuals after good order has been restored."

The Chair of Trustees then asked, "What would you do to raise exam attainments?"

"As you must all know, Eydon Vale's average for five or more good GCSEs for the last fifteen years has been 15 per cent. Ofsted thought the 'Progress 8' scores were catastrophic. At both of the extremes of the ability range, its value-added scores were in the bottom 2 per cent for the country. Where to start? I would invite the parents of the Year 11 pupils with the top quarter of forecast grades to attend an interview at the school on the last night of this term or the first night of next. They would be asked to give their permission for their children to attend 'catch-up' classes in the core subjects for one hour after school every night and Saturday mornings. We would also run an Easter School.

"The targeted pupils would be told these are compulsory. Other Year 11s may attend with their parents' permission. The parents would be told that each targeted pupil would have a named mentor, who will contact them twice a week. This would not be a friendly chat. They would guide the pupils' progress, homework and revision. Parents, mentors and pupils would then sign a contract. In this way, I would hope to reach the median national score on value added by the summer."

"And the least able?" asked the third Parent Governor. "Ofsted were, if anything, more critical of this than any other aspect of Eydon Vale's performance."

"I would not dispute this for a moment, but I would argue that this is a historical failing in English education. As Heads of Ofsted constantly observe, we are effectively giving our more vulnerable pupils a 'life sentence'. Unsatisfactory progress, semi-literacy and limited exam results mean lifelong poverty and early death. Without a coordinated, national, training programme for children with special needs, this is bound to happen.

"If I were appointed, I would set up courses for a core group of staff as reading and writing coaches, as soon as their GCSE classes leave. Then they could start work for two or three lessons per week next September. At the same time, I would negotiate with the Head of Eydon Vale's Special Unit to see if that core group could teach a few lessons in there each week, to prepare for the day when the pupils from the unit could be integrated. We would start to make Eydon Vale a more inclusive school in six months' time."

The final question came from the third Parent Governor. She asked, "Why volunteer for a new challenge like taking a school like Eydon Vale out of special measures, when most senior managers of your age are planning their retirement?"

"My daughter asked me the very same question yesterday morning. My answer is because I refuse to accept that this generation of Eydon Vale pupils is lost!"

A week after my appointment, HMI returned and failed Eydon Vale. Rhiannon intimated that a special staff meeting had been convened for 3.15 the next day. John Silver told me I could take the afternoon off to attend. When I arrived, the hall was half full. The sight of the teachers momentarily disoriented me. I mistook them for poor parents, weighed down by debt, withered by family problems and unloved by their children. Jonathon Milton, whom I later found to be one of the most impressive classroom practitioners, looked particularly sombre. His back was bent. He looked exhausted and bowed by the weight of failure.

Sir Henry Robinson was chairing the meeting. He told the staff that the verdict of April's Ofsted Inspection had been updated. Eydon Vale was no longer seen as just having "serious weaknesses" but was now in "special measures". HMI would be deciding its future within the fortnight.

Sir Henry went on to explain just how badly Eydon Vale's children were underachieving. Their Junior Schools scores suggested there was little difference between their ability and that of the children in two other schools in Holmesside. These had got at least 40% to pass five or more GCSEs at A-C grades. For the last fifteen years, Eydon Vale had averaged 15%. Schools in other Local Authorities with far higher levels of poverty were getting better results.

When I came back with this news, John Silver commiserated. From that point through to the Christmas holidays, he generously gave me leave to spend a day a week as part of his support for colleagues in a failing school. I am sure he would also have allowed me to withdraw my resignation, but I was determined to see things through. I spent these Wednesdays teaching, walking the corridors and discussing the Action Plan with Rhiannon.

That first Wednesday, I felt as if I was in a time warp. It was just like being back at Tulse Hill as a probationary teacher. Controlling every class was a battle. The experience of teaching even a single lesson was totally disorienting. It took me three days' successful lessons at Rectory Road before I could reassure myself that I had not lost my touch.

Brian Smithson, the Assistant Head in charge of Discipline and Attendance, took me around the school on that first Wednesday. He had a mild way of addressing the children, but the way he approached the large groups of wandering pupils reminded me of a cool-headed full-back in Rugby Union, making a "mark" in the face of an attacking pack. He would call the children to him, make them line up against the wall, calm them down, and then direct them to their lesson. Though they were respectful to his face, they never stayed in their classes for long, though. To them, it was a game.

At break time that first Wednesday, I took on the top corridor and Brian the ground floor. I did not see any other staff on duty, as Brian had asked, and there were many children still milling around. I was wearing a homemade nametag, which read *Mr J. Shaw, new Deputy Head*, and I acted the part as energetically as I could. This did not appear to impress the wanderers. Four boys refused outright to do as I told them, and I had to remove them to a private office to tell them how severe the consequences would be if they disobeyed me again.

That second Wednesday, when I got to Eydon Vale, I was given my real badge of office: a set of keys. It was essential for me to get back in the classroom again and prove myself. I also needed to see for myself what the pupils were capable of. It was the pupils with the greatest potential who appeared to have suffered most from the previous regime, so I asked if I could take the top stream Year 11 English class. Gillian Newsome, the pupil who had asked how I would deal with bullying at the interview, was in that group and I was anxious about what she had said about her lack of GCSE English coursework.

I had decided to prepare them for a mock exam question on the GCSE Anthology: Letter *from Yorkshire*. My credibility was in the balance. Establishing boundaries with my own top set and special needs classes was essential if I was to win over the staff. So, when five pupils arrived late for my first lesson with Year 11 at Eydon Vale, I was draconian. I lined them up at the front of the classroom and surveyed them with a death stare. "From now on, you will all arrive on time, with homework at the ready. Next lesson, the last person to come through that door will be sanctioned. We do not have a moment to lose. As the top set, you will have to be the pacemakers for the rest of the school.

"I shall be taking you through to your GCSEs. From January until May, you will be receiving written homework twice a week. I shall also be leading your catch-up classes in English every Monday evening. And this weekend, I shall be here for your Saturday morning lesson. Your parents have all signed contracts, giving their consent. These extra lessons are not voluntary. I expect all of you to be here on time. If I suspect you have gone to your Saturday job, I shall phone your employer there and then."

That first lesson was not a success. What was clear, though, was that I was going to be incredibly strict. However, I also emphasised the importance of intellectual freedom. "You will learn at least as much from each other as from me," I told them. "My view of literature will reflect my life experience, but yours will mirror a teenager's. A 50-year old's reading will be different from a 15 year old's; a boy's from a girl's. We will start by practising reading aloud. Each of you, in turn, will read a short section of this poem. Then I shall wait until one of you makes a comment or asks me a question. I shall be looking for perceptive readings. You will teach each other how to think.

"Everyone in the class will learn to make at least one comment every lesson. English is not like any other subject. In Physics and History, it takes years of study to become an expert, but anyone of your age can get to the heart of a poem, provided that you read it carefully and reflect on it with full attention. What I want is for someone to ask me a question to which I don't know the answer or make a comment which I have never heard before. I know it's hard, especially the first time, but I want you to jump off that cliff! Now, who would like to read the first section of 'Letters from Yorkshire'?"

I had a long wait before anyone dared to say anything. The class felt threatened. Other pupils could be heard running down the corridors, scuffling, laughing and shouting out my newly coined nickname. I could even catch a glimpse of them through the corridor windows. No wonder so many staff were absent with neck and backache, if their attention was constantly being distracted by the twenty or more internal truants wandering the corridors.

At the end of the lesson, I found about a dozen children on the corridor, many of them with no proper explanation. I had brought along a small red notebook and wrote down the children's names, Year Groups and excuses. At the end of break, I went to the main staircase on the ground floor, and a group of five Year 11 boys surrounded me, jostling and swearing. They ignored my questions about where they should be and my requests that they should give me their names. There were no other teachers to be seen. Eventually, the boys ran off down the corridors, shouting and laughing.

I caught up with them a few minutes later, and this time Angela Clayton, a Teacher Governor, arrived to help. She told me the pupils' names and they then followed me to a nearby office. Brian Smithson now appeared and kept the bulk of the group outside, while I interviewed each one individually. A red-faced, Year 8 boy called Jake Sangster told me quite bluntly that he knew why I had been hired. It was "to turn the school round".

He said that he liked the school as it was though, and he did not think I would win. His tone was amiable and objective, but his attitude was that of a deliberate and conscious mutineer. I told each of them that for swearing at me and refusing my requests, my recommendation was that they should be excluded for seven school days, then only allowed to return on a behaviour contract. They were not impressed.

At a meeting with Rhiannon and Brian, I discovered that there had been a riot in the previous week. After the staff had heard that Eydon Vale had failed its inspection, 30 staff called in sick. Groups of 50 children ran around the building, whooping and banging on doors. An empty Art Room had been ransacked. A chair had been thrown through a window so violently that it had dislodged the frame. A sack of dry plaster of Paris and some solvent had been thrown down the staircase outside and a hapless Year 11 boy heaved over a bannister. HMI had heard about this and put Eydon Vale into the sub-category of Special Measures called "Turbulent Schools". Though none of us knew this at the time, this allowed the Secretary of State to close the school at a moment's notice for fear of riot.

Rhiannon, Brian and I agreed that if we were to make a start on disciplinary reform this term, he and I would have to call a meeting of the five Heads of Year. This was to lay the foundations for one of the most important changes we were likely to put into place for the school's survival. The only item on the agenda was an open discussion of the strengths and weaknesses of Eydon Vale's present discipline system. Having visited virtually every class in the school, it seemed to me that the central issue was how we could empower class teachers. I told them that my main aim was to build a safer, more secure school, zone by zone.

I floated my idea of two full day's training on behavioural management on the last day of this term and the first day of the Easter Term. Given the state of discipline in the classroom, it seemed to me that the teacher's prime responsibility was to get children to listen to them. Staff, who did not know how to do this, had a simple choice: either learn or leave.

Brian stopped me to ensure that everyone understood the seriousness of what I was saying. He asked me if this was what I was going to tell the staff on the training day. I told him there was no alternative but to be forthright. I assured everyone that it would be essential for every single member of staff to understand that all our jobs depended on everyone getting every class to listen and learn.

I then asked the group their opinion about how many staff could actually do this and how many could not. There was a long and painful silence. Eventually, Brian said that there were probably 30 permanent teachers who could and about 15 who could not. There were also about seven substitute teachers working in the school at any given time. One or two were excellent, but most had serious problems. There were also seven recent recruits, all Newly Qualified Teachers, on the staff, and most of them were still learning the basic skills of classroom control. He calculated that 54% had poor discipline.

Brian's honesty cleared the air. At this point, it became obvious that I was in earnest and that the Heads of Year would support me. It was an exhilarating meeting and what made it so productive was to have such an unambiguous answer, given the mystery about how the school had got into such difficulties. According to the Heads of Year, the previous Head had lacked focus. He had let himself be pulled in different directions by the staff, the parents, the LEA and the Department of Education.

One Head of Year asked me how I would justify excluding children, in the light of the government's inclusion policies. I explained that I used to lead Rectory Road's exclusion panels and knew how destructive they could be. However, we were in an extremely precarious situation. The disorderliness of a few children was damaging the education of the many.

The other Heads of Year joined in, warning me how much pressure the LEA had put on the previous Head to minimise exclusions. There had been no official suspensions for two years. I argued that for schools in special measures, the key audience was not the LEA but the Inspectors. Inclusion was not a simple issue. We had to think about the children from the special unit in their wheelchairs. They had rights, too. There may well be a time when Eydon Vale could become a more inclusive school, but we would not be considering this for another term at least.

It was only at the close of the discussion that Brian admitted that while the previous Head had not formally excluded anyone in two years, 230 children had been informally "sent home" during the first 60 days of the Christmas Term. This was an astronomical figure, symptomatic of a complete breakdown in good order. It could be compared to three fixed-term exclusions at Rectory Road, my present, more disadvantaged school!

My breakthrough with the top set Year 11s came on that third Wednesday. Half the class was in a French oral exam, but the remainder were on time. I reminded them of the five new rules, then asked them to turn to the most sexually explicit poem in the anthology: Andrew Marvell's 'To His Coy Mistress'.

"The rhyme on the word 'breast' makes it sound so palpable, but there's also a sense of bathos," commented the forthright Elroy Samson. "Marvell's being witty at his own expense. He's saying there's a fat chance he'll ever caress it. He's just like us, a frustrated teen at heart." Despite the noise of internal truants clattering down the corridor, the group's concentration was intense.

Not wanting to be outdone, Gillian Newsome put her hand up next. "You speak for yourself. If the woman of Andrew Marvell's dreams were indeed 'coy', the physicality of the rhyme would scare her off. He is never going to send this poem to a real woman. Not if he has any sense, that is." Half a dozen hands went up when we started the second section of the poem:

> But at my back I always hear
> Time's winged chariot hurrying near

"I agree with Gillian," Ming Lee commented. "Marvell was writing a hypothetical argument, not a love poem to a real woman. "There's the link between the structure of 'Coy Mistress' and the imagery of 'Letters from Yorkshire'. Both are about virtual reality. The woman in this poem doesn't exist. Marvell is not addressing her. She's an avatar, and he's writing a witty academic argument, designed to appeal to his male friends. Marvell's composed the poem to be read out loud to them at the university bar."

There were fierce arguments about whether the image of a graveyard embrace was morbid. Alice proved the most articulate: "Marvell is using his apparent desire for this probably quite ordinary young woman to tell us something existential. Life is precious and over so quickly. Faced with death's 'iron gates', we have to grab our opportunities while we can!"

Elroy, Gillian, Ming Lee and Alice went on to lead the transformation of Eydon Vale's exam results.

On the fourth Wednesday, I asked the top set to write an essay comparing "Letters" and "Coy Mistress" Considering this was the first time they had been asked to write a timed essay, their concentration was quite good. Some of them had had to be reminded, "Don't stop to think, keep writing", but when I marked their essays, there was a fair sprinkling of top grades. Most were at 4 or 5 – borderline passes. Interaction between the pupils and myself had so far been very formal, but as they left the room, several of them said, "Thank you".

At first, I could not quite believe my ears. This was a new experience for me. My Year 11 comprehensive pupils had normally been far too *cool* to thank their teachers, except perhaps sarcastically. But these were simply grateful that a teacher was preparing them for exam conditions at last. On my way down the corridors that morning, a smattering of applause followed me. At first, it was unnerving. But it developed into a divisive and ominous game. Even though I punished the children and summoned their parents, some Year 8 lads carried on chanting the word, "Respect!" at me, every time they saw Rhiannon and me together.

At early morning briefing on the fifth Wednesday, I asked the staff to send representatives from each of their tutor groups for a meeting of the school council. In the event, only the Year 11s, Year 9s and Year 7s turned up. My aim was for the pupils to help clarify the issues about positive reinforcers for the new disciplinary system. The group quickly developed their own lists of preferred rewards. They had clear opinions and were surprisingly skilful at resolving differences.

Alice Lawton's younger sister Katie had always wanted to become a primary school teacher. Like her mother, who served as a Parent Representative on the board that had just appointed me, Katie Lawton was an articulate and forthright feminist. According to her mother, Katie asked to be her form representative on the council meeting that morning. It was the first time it had met in all the time that Katie had been at Eydon Vale. We started with introductions and I asked if the Head's PA, Edwina Brown, could take notes of all they said.

They were then asked about the existing discipline policy. Katie declared the existing school rules "far too vague. Take the first instruction: 'Show respect for one another'. Of course, it would be great if all the pupils were more polite to one another. That rule is not going to make kids consider others' feelings, though. It's like telling them to be perfect. In the real world, Year 7s like us need protection. If a rule is going to work, it must be more precise: a command, like keep your hands to yourself or get your homework in on time. It must reward the pupil who carries it out and punish the pupil who gets it wrong."

There was a general agreement from the other children. "Good teachers have clear boundaries," Katie went on unabashed. "They know what they will or will not accept. And, if the kids are going to learn how to behave, the rules need to be much more practical. There ought to be something like doggie snacks for those who work hard and the naughty step for the bullies."

"The reason I've called you here today is to ask your help with the doggie snacks idea," I replied. "I want to create a rewards policy for the New Year and I need you to tell me what the pupils at Eydon Vale would prefer. Last week, I went around some of the classes here. I am convinced that there are lots of kids just like you, who want to get on, but whose needs are ignored. It's the misbehaving minority, who get the teachers' attention.

"Some of them no doubt need it, but most get far too much of it for their own good. What Eydon Vale needs is a set of rewards for pupils who can sit still, write at length in silence or join in discussions in a thoughtful, constructive way. So, we need a menu of rewards that teach the little things like facing their teachers and listening to instructions, as well as the big things like winning the football cup."

"Lollipops for the teachers' pets?" smiled Pete Sangster, a bright Year 11, who had been demoted to second streams for cheeking teachers and fighting.

"I can see what you're driving at," said Gillian Newsome, who had heard all about Guided Discipline as a member of the pupil panel that had interviewed me. "But don't you think that good work should be its own reward, sir?"

"You know how important those GCSE grades are better than anyone, Gillian," I replied. " *You* will succeed in life, whatever reward system we employ. But that's not true of most of your peers. What I think is this: unless we get a dramatic improvement in behaviour and exam results, Eydon Vale will close. In an ideal world, we would not need extrinsic rewards. But Eydon Vale is not a perfect world. We have to set up a system that has traction."

Not to be outshone by her sister's friend, Katie said, "Lollipops won't work. They are naff. If the rewards are going to work, they have to reflect what the pupils like."

"Absolutely," I agreed. "This is what I have called you together to discuss today. I need your help. You will have all seen the new building down the road. It's going to be called the New Fydon. There could be a wonderful future inside it for the children of this area. And what you suggest today could make that future a reality. So, what would actually make Year 7s like you want to behave?"

"Those salty, chewy, caramel bars," interrupted a Year 7 boy. "What do you call them?"

"Rulers," said a Year 7 girl.

"Pens," said a third. "And fizzy drinks."

"And sketchbooks and pencil cases..."

"You could send letters sent to parents congratulating them on their kids' work."

47

"A set of Bronze, Silver and Gold Certificates sent home like we had at Primary School."

"A special celebration assembly for the kids who got the most gold certificates?" asked Katie.

"None of the parents would come. They are all at work," pointed out one Year 9 pupil.

"Better if we had McDonalds vouchers and tickets for the cinema, or a Man United game," grumbled another pupil from Year 9.

"Have you got all that, Edwina?" I asked the PA.

"You are doing so well," Edwina Brown said to the School Council.

"All these little prizes ... they are no good. What would really turn the kids on is a big prize – like a motorbike," returned Pete Sangster, to obvious nods from the older boys. "We could have a lottery every week, a lucky dip. Everyone who has been good gets a ticket for the big draw."

Katie was irrepressible. She calmly pointed out that this was neither fair nor helpful. "The work of good individuals will never be recognised if the prizes are given out as a lottery. If the rewards were few and dependent on chance, this could have a negative effect on the great majority of pupils, who want to support the teachers. There are lots of kids who long for quiet, and who are fazed by the noise and chaos. It's kids like them who need rewarding. Their little, everyday acts like concentrating in class, going the extra mile with homework and opening the door to a kid in a wheelchair need to be recognised."

"So, Katie, what you are proposing is that we have a variety of small prizes, not a lottery. Can I put that to the vote?" I asked.

Katie nodded.

"Can I ask the secretary to read back the list of prizes the Council had mentioned?" I suggested.

After Edwina reminded the representatives of these, I asked, "Are there any you'd like to add?"

"Mints," said one Year 7.

"Chocolates," another.

"Great. All in favour of the small prizes that the Head's PA has listed with the new additions, please raise your right hands," I declared. The disproportionately large numbers of Year 7s enthusiastically supported Katie's proposal, and when the older pupils saw they were in the minority, they sheepishly followed. There was a second vote on Pete Sangster's motion for Prize Draws, and this time it was outvoted.

Finally, I asked for a resolution to take to the Board of Trustees. Gillian Newsome's suggestion was this: "At its meeting on the 14th November, the School Council agreed not to award Prize Draws in the future. We will inaugurate a menu of rewards that would reinforce the little things that helped make for a more orderly school, like facing the teacher and listening to instructions, going the extra mile with homework and opening the door to a kid in a wheelchair."

"If that is acceptable," I smiled to nods from the pupils, "I will go to the trustees and ask them for a grant of £4000 per term in small prizes and merit slips. Does anyone have any comments or questions, before I close the meeting?"

"Yes, I have," said Katie. "Do you have the guts to stand up to the bad lads, Mr Shaw?"

Chapter Four: Courage

As I walked down Eydon Vale's corridors on the last Wednesday of that Christmas Term, one of the internal truants shouted, "Shaw's coming." They ran away when they saw me. By now, most of the children knew that I would mean business. A solitary Year 9 who had been sent out of class was brazenly punching the safety glass in a fire alarm, however. When confronted, he threw a tantrum. Not without difficulty, I escorted him to my new office in the school foyer to calm down. He reminded me of a pupil called Joseph Samuda, who was in my first form group at Tulse Hill. I learned more from Joseph about managing children in extremis than any textbook. Joseph learned little from me, though, and was indicted years later for murder.

That afternoon there was a meeting in Rhiannon's office. She wanted to review our new disciplinary strategy. With her were Margaret Clinton, an educational psychologist with experience of Assertive Discipline and Marina O'Rourke, from one of the neighbouring LEA's Behaviour Support Services. Rhiannon told Mary and Margaret about the issues raised by the HMI visit and the subsequent riot. Margaret and I then briefed Mary and Rhiannon on the best way to introduce Guided Discipline in a failing school. We ended by agreeing on the outline of a two-term, 14-hour in-service training programme for all staff.

After school that night, there was a follow up meeting for the Heads of Year and the Special Support Assistants who ran Eydon Vale's two behaviour support bases. They were desperate to know how safe their jobs were. I told them I saw them as the backbone of the school. They now had to act as if they knew we would come through. I passed on to our plans for the training course, zoning and the behavioural bases for the internal truants. There was much hilarity about the loss of their old, shared office and transfer to their new zones, but they were keen to embrace a more strategic role.

The final Thursday morning at Rectory Road was painful. As well as one teacher holding onto my coat and begging me not to go, the parent of one of our most gifted pupils came into school to make a personal plea for me not to let her son down. At Eydon Vale, there had been a pantomime in the hall, an excuse for egg and flour fights throughout the school. There must have been twenty pupils covered in flour. Five or six children greeted me warmly as I made my way in. Several others, including a boy whom I had already threatened with exclusion, wished me "Merry Christmas".

The Head's Personal Assistant had contacted the parents of the 55 targeted pupils in Year 11. She had also collated all their mock exam results and attendance records. Rhiannon had drafted a contract, which outlined our commitment to provide "catch-up classes" five nights a week, on Saturday mornings and during the school holidays, plus a mentor for each targeted pupil. The mentor would see each of their pupils once a week and contact the parents afterwards. The new classes were to be compulsory. The targeted children would have to promise to attend, keep up with their homework and coursework and revise. The parents would have to promise to check the homework and their children's homework diaries.

We asked the 55 targeted pupils and their parents to come in on the last Thursday of the Christmas term at hourly intervals from 2 till 7 o'clock. Six parents deferred their appointments until the first day of the next term and 42 turned up. Nine "Assertive Mentors" interviewed them individually. Our conditions were strict. The children would have to give up their Saturday jobs. The parents would have to find someone else to babysit their younger siblings after school. No one could take a term-time holiday and get the grades. No one would be allowed to attend these classes without a contract. Our only sanctions for parents and children who broke the contract would be to remove the assertive mentoring service. There was some anger that the children seemed to have been given no homework before their mock exams, but all the parents present signed the contract.

As agreed with the Trustees, Eydon Vale was shut on the last Friday of the term for whole staff training. Rhiannon opened proceedings. She told them the news she had just been given. As a result of November's Inspection, the Secretary of State for Education had redesignated Eydon Vale as a "turbulent school". He had reserved powers to close the school at a moment's notice in case of riot. He had asked the Home Office to ensure that the Local Constabulary now counted any request for assistance as the highest priority. An observer would be visiting the school three times a week. Rhiannon concluded by telling the staff she was sure that we could make the rapid and radical changes needed, especially in terms of school discipline. After her preamble, I introduced Guided

Discipline. Everything was based on prior experience, particularly of Lee Canter's Assertive Discipline:

There ought to be a national training programme for such low frequency/ high-risk events, to ensure that all teachers are ready to work in schools as turbulent as this. But the sad truth is that few are prepared for coping in schools like Eydon Vale. One of the major problems with our initial teacher training in this country is the lack of detail in the management of pupil behaviour. When I was teaching at a University Department of Education, I used to ask the PGCE students what were their biggest issues. The main thing they really wanted to know more about was school discipline.

When I discovered this, I started giving seminars to leadership teams on disciplinary reform. In order to become effective, teachers first needed to ask themselves radical questions about what they were doing in the classroom. Was it to teach their subjects? Was it because they were an authority in that subject? If so, they had to take the existential decision that they were going to be the boss in their own classrooms. They had to carry with them an air of certainty, whatever they might feel inside.

So, it followed that they had to accept their responsibility for teaching students how to behave. They had to convince the pupils that they did mean business. They had to establish clear rules for the classroom. They had to communicate those rules to the students, and they had to teach the students how to follow them. Thirdly, they had to master the skill of positive reinforcement. For every single item of blame, they had to learn to praise 20 or more kinds of desirable pupil behaviour. This is easier said than done, but it is essential. There is no doubt in my mind: positive reinforcers provide the real engine of behavioural change across a school, not sanctions.

At the moment, far too many teachers and pupils believe that good discipline springs from negative consequences, demerits or detentions. That interpretation is wrong. It simply does not work. The key to good discipline is catching students being good: recognising and supporting them when they behave appropriately and letting them know you like it, day in and day out, year after year.

However, when students choose to break the rules, effective teachers have no hesitation in using firm and consistent sanctions. As one of my ex-pupils put it, 'Good teachers have clear boundaries.' These sanctions are not necessarily very heavy. A nod or a look from an assertive teacher can bring a class back into line. But if the situation warrants, effective teachers need also to be extremely direct, or as another of my ex-pupils put it, 'In your face.'

For my teaching practice, I went to an extremely down-at-heel boys' secondary modern school in one of London's red-light districts. Most days only half the pupils on the register ever turned up. Gangs of children constantly wandered the corridors and concentration levels were as poor as here. Most other teachers in the building had disciplinary problems. One day, though, as I was exploring the school, I walked in on a lesson given by the Deputy Head. He spoke in a quiet but penetrating voice and the class seemed to drink in every word he said.

The scales fell from my eyes. I suddenly realised what a fool I had been. There is no point coming to school as a teacher unless you can teach. And you cannot teach unless the pupils listen. I had to learn how to enforce a culture of listening or get out of the job. The other thing I realised with a jolt was that even though this deputy was an effective teacher, he wasn't doing his job. If he could do it, why wasn't he passing on these skills?

A better deputy would have ensured that all the teachers in a school had a discipline plan. This should have included an agreed list of rules, plus another list of 101 desirable behaviours that a teacher can praise. And it ought to have explained exactly what would happen when students chose to misbehave. All students need to know what to expect in the classroom. The teachers need to discuss aspects of this plan through every PSHE lesson. They need to drill the class in the rules every lesson.

Without a plan, we tend to be inconsistent. One day we may ignore students who are talking, wandering the corridors, or disrupting the class. The next day we sanction students for the same behaviours. An effective discipline plan has to be applied fairly to all students at all times. Any student who deliberately disrupts the class and stops the teacher from teaching will suffer the same consequence. And a written plan should be sent home to parents, so everyone knows what the school's standards are and what the consequences would be if students choose to misbehave. When a teacher calls a parent, there should be no surprises.

A good discipline plan should include a maximum of five clear rules. It should have a menu of rewards that the pupils in the school accept and want. And each school must choose the consequences with which the staff are comfortable. For example, the first time a student breaks a rule, the student is reminded of the rule. The second infraction brings a warning, which is copied onto a tracking sheet on the teacher's desk.

The demarcation lines for temporary and permanent exclusions must be unambiguous. Corporal punishment should never be administered. Even the most innocent touching can be wrongly interpreted by Social Workers and litigious parents. The golden rule for everyone at Eydon Vale from this moment on is that if you are ever tempted to invade a child's space, you are to put your hands in your pockets. I hope that's agreed?

That said, we teachers have the right to determine what is best for our pupils, and to expect compliance. None of our pupils should ever prevent us from teaching or keep another student from learning again. To accomplish this, we must all act more assertively. Assertive teachers act confidently and quickly in situations that require behaviour management. They have a few clearly stated classroom rules and give firm, clear, concise directions to students who require control. Students who comply are reinforced, whereas those who disobey rules and directions receive negative consequences.

Assertive teachers build positive, trusting relationships with their students and teach appropriate classroom behaviour to those who don't show it at present. They are demanding, yet warm in interaction and supportive of the pupils. Respect and responsibility are essential. Assertive teachers listen carefully to what their students have to say, speak respectfully to them, and treat everyone fairly. Assertive teachers do not see students as adversaries, nor do they use an abrasive or sarcastic style. Neither are they unassertive: by which I mean timid, inconsistent, or non-directive.

Guided Discipline stands or falls by the way positive reinforcement is policed. That is my foremost objective as your deputy head. I will visit all of you in all your classrooms twice a week. I will give everyone the Guided Discipline observation schedule and immediate feedback. I have no intention of embarrassing you, blaming you or catching you out. I want to catch you being good. And you will all be welcome to observe my lessons.

Some of you will be thinking that this is worse than Ofsted. But Ofsted never asks permission to enter your domain. If you don't want me to come in at that moment, show me your palm. It may be that a kid is in the middle of a complex explanation, or another is fooling around, and you don't want to be embarrassed. I quite understand. I will come back later that morning.

I will never tell you, 'Your discipline is hopeless, you never recapitulate the rules, you are not giving enough rewards.' I will pick out ten good points and set one target. I spent a lot of time with one of the failing teachers at Rectory Road. In the beginning, she was wholly inadequate, and by the time she left, her discipline was quite satisfactory. I tried every trick in the book to teach her the competencies. When she left, she sent me a card, thanking me for my kindness. In her new job in a less demanding school, Ofsted told her she'd become a good teacher. But I was not trying to be kind. I just showered her with positive reinforcement for everything she'd got right.

One of the most gifted pupils on the School Council was adamant that children should not need rewards to behave properly. In orderly schools, this may be true. But it seems to me from my visits to Eydon Vale that one of our knottiest problems is going to be ridding the school of low-level disruption. Even when we have sorted out the really dramatic issues like physical violence and bullying, we are probably going to have to spend a lot of time on this. But praise, reinforcement and rewards have a crucial role in teaching everyday competencies like listening to staff.

Ofsted inspectors never carry out demonstration lessons, of course. Whereas you should feel free to come knocking on my door any day. And from time to time I shall be making videos of my demonstration classes. The one I shall be showing after coffee was made with one of Eydon Vale's Year 8 groups last week, many of whom have significant learning difficulties. At the start of the lesson, I put two rules up on the board: 'Keep negative comments to yourself' and 'Listen to staff and follow directions'. We chanted the rules.

Then I asked them to tell me what they thought the rules meant and said 'Great!' or 'Well done' to every student who got it right. Those who helped me explain the lesson objectives I had previously written on the board were also praised. I praised details from the pupils' previous work. As they settled to the writing task, I counted heads down and said, 'I can see one, two, three, four, five pupils working already.'

When we did have a moment of absolute silence, I asked the class to put their pens down and tell me what they could hear. When they replied, 'Nothing, it's quiet!' I gave them a point towards a class merit. After 10 minutes, I asked them to tell me how many words they had written and distributed merits to those who were trying hardest.

The quality of courage that it takes to implement Guided Discipline is in my view, quite distinctive. It is active and focused. It's like the strength of mind of a frontline infantryman. Concentration on the task at hand is a matter of life and death to them. My father trained with the Special Boat Squadron. He said that when his life and that of his platoon came under threat, he would focus all his attention on the objective he had set himself. If he was hurt or if a comrade fell, he would ignore it. He would blot it out of his mind.

'Keep moving forward,' he would tell me. 'Don't be distracted. If you stop and stare, even for a moment, you become an easy target. Your squad will be confused, and they will lose momentum. Just seeing your determination encourages your unit and discourages the enemy. So, don't be put off. Don't let yourself be shocked or surprised. Hood your eyes, so they only see the objective. Muffle your ears, so all you hear are the orders you give and receive.'

What we find when we put Guided Discipline into effect is that our experience of the here and now intensifies. For most of your life, you will have thought in terms of good days and bad days, good years and bad years. As soon as you start to implement this new disciplinary code, you will realise that life is actually made up of good quarters of an hour and bad quarters of an hour. The bad moments, the panics and the rages: they pass. Let them go. Don't let yourself stare into the abyss.

The main point of this training is to instil a belief in everyone that there is no alternative: you have to be the boss in your own classroom. Through every interaction, you will be emphasising that you will not back away. I tell every class I teach: 'This is my domain! In my classroom, you follow my directions.' Whenever I feel tired or lacking in energy, I tell myself, 'You are the only adult in this situation. It is in the interests of the children that you set the agenda, and you define their boundaries.' That goes right to the top of the organisation. The Senior Leadership Team always has to have 'the power to overawe'.

This is deadly serious. Turning round a school like Eydon Vale is a mean business. But we have to mean business. Our jobs depend on it. Guided Discipline works best when all staff work together. Each of us has to learn to become assertive in our own classrooms. Each of us had to play our part. Nobody can afford to let the rest of the staff down. We have to do it for our personal survival. We are all alone together. The sooner we learn how to use all the positive reinforcers, rules and sanctions, the sooner we get Ofsted off our backs.

This speech led to half an hour of quick-fire debate. A Swedish supply teacher said that what I proposed was too authoritarian for him. He handed in his notice and left that afternoon. No one else made any serious challenge, however. I distributed the stack of books on Guided Discipline that the Governors had purchased for each member of staff. "Read them over the holidays. Read every page. Don't let me down. "The first day of next term, we will decide the rules and sanctions."

After coffee, I showed one of Lee Canter's films and gave a brief talk about our other priority: raising the standards of the more able pupils. I emphasised that 40% of Eydon Vale pupils were capable of what used to be called 5+ A-Cs and that even at this late stage, Rhiannon and I did think we could reach 30% in two terms. If discipline improved, this ought to be enough to get the school out of special measures.

The last piece of work I asked the staff to do was watch a clip from the film about the deliverance of an American School which was about to lose its accreditation: *Stand and Deliver.* Term ended with a staff Christmas lunch, for which Rhiannon had brought wine and soft drinks.

Chapter Five: Securing the Bridgehead

The Trustees closed Eydon Vale for teacher training for the last day of the Christmas term and the first day of the Easter Term. It would reopen on a phased basis, starting with the Year 11s. Most of the staff had read at least one of the books on Guided Discipline during the holiday. Unfortunately, the central heating had broken down. Even though the Hall was freezing, Rhiannon decided we should carry on as planned.

Graham Ironsides, the Head of Holme House School, gave the inaugural address. He and Bea Wright were the best-known exponents of Assertive Discipline when we were thinking of adapting its approach for Rectory Road. He was a courageous, honest and independent-minded Head, who talked in terms of "campaigns" and had a flair for looking after his "troops". Nineteen years previously, when Holme House had failed one of the very first Ofsted Inspections, the *Sunday Times* had run a damning article about the school.

The Holme House estate was one of poorest in Northern England. Over half the pupils were eligible for Free School Meals. The *Sunday Times* had included graphic pictures of boarded-up council houses, idle shipyards and poor families. When Graham took over, his Year 7 intake was 85. It was now 200 and he told the staff at Eydon Vale that Assertive Discipline had laid the foundations for that recovery.

After showing us a PowerPoint of his five simple rules, his rewards and sanctions, he told us there was no magic powder that he could sprinkle. Each of us had to learn the routines for ourselves, show the children that we meant what we said, catch them when they were being good and use positive reinforcement. If we acted consistently, there would be an immediate and long-term improvement in the pupils' behaviour.

Assertive Discipline by itself would not raise standards of pupil attainment, however. He had had to set up extra classes for targeted Year 11 pupils and these had raised the proportion of pupils getting 5+ A-Cs from under 10% to the equivalent of 38% over these nineteen years. His school had been one of the poorest in the country, and yet its value-added was one of the highest. His talk was enthusiastically received.

The staff then split into their 10 zonal groups, which more or less corresponded with academic subjects. Each group was asked to sort out a buddy system for mutual support in each zone and review one aspect of Guided Discipline, such as the rules, rewards or sanctions. The administrative group started planning who would do which aspects of the data gathering, record keeping and communication with parents. There was a lively debate within each of the groups. The first to report back was the classroom rules group.

After coffee, their proposals were thrown open to the whole staff. I emphasised that this would be their last chance to amend the rules. If there were any good reason to object, they should say so now; otherwise, they should henceforth hold their peace. We then passed onto the corridor rules. When these were thrown open to the whole staff, the changes were more substantial.

A small number of changes were made to the menu of sanctions. It took us two and a half hours to agree on the system, at which point we stopped for a free lunch. I reminded the staff that I would give them a week to learn these new strategies and then carry out the first of my classroom visits. This was not a philosophical exercise. It was a battle for the survival of the school and their jobs. The best way for them to learn was for me to observe them at work and give them individual guidance.

There was considerable satisfaction with the morning's work. What cheered the staff particularly was the extent to which they had been consulted about our new disciplinary procedures, particularly on exclusions. In the afternoon Marina O'Rourke from the LEA's Behaviour Support Services showed us a range of powerful videos and PowerPoint presentations on Guided Discipline. She kept stopping the tapes to re-emphasise the practical details.

It was a battle with the cold, and we had to finish early. The admin staff created posters for the menus of rules, rewards and sanctions, to be distributed around all the classrooms, stairwells and corridors before the next morning. The new term was to start with a staged re-entry: Year 11 on Tuesday, Years 10 and 11 on Wednesday and so on, until the school was complete on Friday. Each day began with an Induction Lesson. New timetables were issued to each pupil. These would let us break up some of the sets that had the greatest behavioural difficulties. The pupils had a worksheet to complete every day on the new rules, rewards and sanctions. Staff were asked to explain how Guided Discipline worked. Then the pupils went to Assemblies where Rhiannon and I reinforced the messages.

When I awoke the second morning of that Easter Term, it was 'Do or die'. This was the moment for which my whole career had been preparing me. I meditated for a few minutes, then drove like a madman to school, so I would arrive pumped full of adrenaline. As the Year 11s filed into the Hall, class by class, I stood at the front, surveying the children with my hardest stare. None of us knew how things would go. We were all completely quiet. The atmosphere was quite unlike anything I had ever experienced. I held the silence for a minute. Then I introduced myself and gave a reading from the third chapter of Ecclesiastes, one of the wisest and most resonant in the Bible.

I am Mr Shaw, the new Deputy Head. I was asked to come here because of my experience in rescuing failing schools. The section from the Old Testament that you just heard: 'There is a time for every purpose under heaven' suggests that each of us will go through times of success and failure. So do schools. Fifteen years ago, Eydon Vale was a good school. More recently, though, behaviour and results have deteriorated. Things will have to improve again. Otherwise, the Government will close us down. They will scatter you and your friends and bulldoze this building. As you heard in the reading, 'There is a time a time to scatter stones and a time to gather them'.

You all know the plans for a new school building. But be under no illusion. The Government would shelve them, shut the school and send you somewhere else at a moment's notice if it felt Eydon Vale was unsafe. Your exam prospects would count for nothing. Many of your hopes and dreams would be lost. Some of your lives would be wrecked.

So, I am telling you that in order to keep your school open, you will have to learn and obey the new rules. If you follow them, you will be rewarded. Your teachers will praise you. We will shower you with chocolate bars, commendation slips, certificates and letters home. The pupils with the most merits will get a pass for the new tuck shop. And if all goes to plan, we'll all be moving into our new school premises.

However, if you choose to break the rules, you will be shown no mercy. I shall be out on the corridors, checking on your behaviour every break and every day. You can also expect me to visit your classrooms two or three times a week.

Eydon Vale is not the first school where I have introduced this discipline code. I can promise that most of you will notice an improvement pretty quickly. You will feel safer and work harder than you have ever worked before. Your exam grades will be higher than you thought possible. My guess is that the Government will give us a month to prove we can do the job. No one expects this to be easy. So, let us bow our heads for a moment of silent reflection about what this day will bring.

In the event, only one pupil had to be given a fixed-term exclusion on that first week. Gary defied one teacher and then jostled his Head of Year. Even as the school refilled, the corridors and playground initially remained clear of internal truants. A retired couple, whose bungalow lay across the school field, phoned Rhiannon to ask if anything was wrong. For the first time in years, they could not hear the racket from the classrooms.

In my first lesson with the top set Year 11 English class, I was quite blunt. The mock exam essays they had written on Romeo and Juliet were not good enough. We also had to complete the reading of Jane Eyre and the poetry anthology. It normally took 52 weeks to do the course. However, we only had 13. This would mean that we would have to stay back after school for three extra lessons a week and come into school at half term and during the Easter holidays. Each day would have the same format. We would read a poem, or a section of a play or novel in its entirety, then slowly in short sections. I would not teach the children anything. They had to make comments and ask me questions.

The pupils would be given feedback using the GCSE Speaking and Listening criteria and excellent effort would be rewarded with praise, commendations and chocolate. No one was to be shy: every offering would be accepted positively. Towards the end of the lesson, the pupils would receive a structured worksheet, which would ensure that none of the major points of the lesson would be neglected. They would then return for one hour after class to write an essay on the poem, chapter or scene under exam conditions.

By now, the pupils seemed to trust me. They understood the situation and accepted the new workload. I forced the issue, however. I told the class I wanted to know whether I had their support. I said I would turn my back. If they believed what I told them, they were to raise their hands. All the children did so. All bar two returned that first night and they wrote in silence for one hour. By the end of the week, all the pupils were turning up and working.

When I arrived 20 minutes early on Saturday with bags of fruit and croissants, several were already waiting outside the gates. Most of the descriptive essays they wrote on their first memories of school – such as Elroy Samson's in this book's Introduction - were still too short. Few scored the higher grades, but there was an excited buzz. Angela Clayton, the Teacher Governor and Acting Head of English, who had taken time out of her weekend to observe me, commented that the children were ready for a change.

Every week the standard of their reading, speaking and listening improved, though it was not until the end of January that Alice Lawton scored our first grade nine. The writing skills took even longer and some of the lessons we did after school on Friday nights were torture for some of the pupils. They desperately wanted to do well. But the effort of writing fast and remembering the sub-skills of spelling and punctuation when they were exhausted gave one of them a headache that lasted weeks.

Every moment that I was not teaching, I visited lessons and carried out structured observations of teachers and the pupils. Blank observation reports were given to the teachers at the start of the week and the pupils were told I was looking to reward their good behaviour and punish the transgressors. Marina O'Rourke, from the LEA's Behaviour Support Services, had obvious expertise in this area and she generously agreed to spend most of January at Eydon Vale, triangulating my observations.

It was clear from the first week of the Easter term that both teachers and pupils wanted the new system to work. Even seasoned staff were intensely nervous about being observed, especially at the start, however. When I stood up at the end of a visit to the Art Department, this startled the member of staff. She was being extremely assertive, measured and calm, but when I told her how well she had done, her reaction was disbelieving. The teachers were still so beaten down, they could not accept they could get things right again.

However, many staff found the introduction of Guided Discipline quite stimulating. Every time I went into the staffroom, I would be asked, "What should I do if....?" As the teacher governor said, "The staff were ready for it!" Students stopped me in the corridors to tell me how much better things were, too. Their attendance and that of the staff improved. The cleaners reported that there was less rubbish on the classroom floors. And the lunch supervisors agreed that the dining halls were quieter.

Adapting the military analogies of Graham Ironside's inaugural address, I told one staff briefing that we were now passing from the "invasion beaches" to "securing the bridgehead". Any slip by any teacher could still bring the whole system down. All the classroom teachers had to discipline themselves and keep to the Guided Discipline script. But at a meeting of the Zone Managers and Duty staff, I insisted they switch off their computer screens during school hours. Our policing of the new system had to be highly visible. They had to keep walking the corridors, so they could catch any colleague who was in danger of slipping.

Old habits were deeply entrenched, though. Managing movement at break and lunchtime proved a particular problem. A system of staggered breaks had grown up under the previous head, with different year groups using the playground at different times. Some staff had been allowing children in early, leaving ownership of the corridors with the children, just when the adults most needed to exercise control. This was giving them ambiguous signals about time boundaries.

The pupils had now been told to come back into school through the doors closest to their next lesson and that they would be kept on the playground until the bells were rung. Each of the playground entrances had double doors, but one of the doors was always locked. The pupils would push against them and every morning some of the younger ones were hurt in the crush.

The staff on playground duty often arrived late, compounding the problem. They frequently felt overcome by the sense of impending violence. So, when a massive, freckle-faced Year 11 student came up to Miss Starr and me on the corridor and told me how much the school had improved, I asked him how he would like to be a prefect. "Why not?" he said.

Miss Starr was scandalised. "You know who that is, don't you? That's Nathan James. He broke a kid's nose last term just for calling him 'gingernut'. His dad's a bouncer at 'The Green Banana'. The whole family's trouble."

At first, the staff were just as sceptical. According to staffroom gossip, Nathan would not miss the opportunity to 'bray' somebody. There were sure to be complaints. I told Nathan and his mate that they were to push open both the double doors and stand in front of them at the moment the bells rang. Sure enough, the children knew better than to shove against a tough guy like Nathan. This simple trick allowed the duty staff to line up the kids and form a queue.

Five minutes work for each morning for the next fortnight transformed movement into school. A look from Nathan immediately quelled the mêlée. Three Year 8s, who failed to grasp the change in ethos, started barging against the teacher on duty, but Nathan backed him up, even giving the teacher their names. They were isolated for the rest of the day and told they would not be readmitted to the school until their parents brought them in the next day.

By the end of that fortnight, the staff had been won over. The ploy had paid off. At the end of his second week as a prefect, I asked Nathan's father to come and see me. Mr James, a huge man, who was wearing only a short-sleeved tee-shirt despite the cold, was obviously expecting to hear the worst. I could hear him growling at Nathan, "I'm not in the mood for any chew tonight, like."

"You don't have to worry, Mr James," I reassured him. "This is not a telling off. I wanted to inform you how well Nathan is doing. He's been a big help. I have appointed him and his friend as my first prefects. They have been helping the teachers clear the yard at break times."

Mr James shook his head in bewilderment and only relaxed as I explained the role Nathan had undertaken in calming the pupils. "Eeee, I allus tried to keep him out of trouble," he explained to his son's embarrassment, "but he niver listens to youse."

"Has he told you about the rewards and merits we have been giving out?" I asked. Mr James took the point immediately. He offered to give Nathan a 'beb' for every merit he won. Mr James was as good as his word. He kept giving Nathan money for every merit that he brought home. The vicious cycle of assaults, suspensions and Governors' Meetings petered out. However, the shock of being singled out for praise in front of his father was too much for Nathan: neither he nor the other bouncers turned up at the doors the next week.

By then, though, the reforms that had been put in place had done their work. The staff were sticking to the agreed time boundaries. The pupils had grown used to queuing in a more orderly manner as they came off the yard. The old ways of behaving had been challenged at the cost of three more temporary suspensions. The pupils could appreciate the improvement, and new norms for movement at the ends of breaks had been established.

The theme I chose for the next week's assemblies was "New Year's Resolutions". Once again, the children listened hard and we focused on Rule Five: "Keep hands, feet, objects and negative remarks to yourself." I told the children about Maria Montessori.

Many years ago, she had set up a school in the toughest part of Naples for the children no one else could teach. The kids were very wild. They didn't know how to behave, so they couldn't learn. They constantly used to argue and squabble, push and fight, run around the room and out of her school.

At first, Maria could not afford tables or chairs for the children. She realised that if they were going to settle, they would all need a safe space of their own. So, she chalked a circle on the floor around each child. All the children were told that this was their space and that no one could enter their space unless the child gave their permission. No one was allowed to be a space invader. Gradually, the children learned to keep their hands, feet and negative comments to themselves.

When I visited Eydon Vale for the first time, I had seen a pupil crying on the corridor because a bigger boy had hit him. I had seen kids pushing and jostling each other. The lunch queues were disorderly and after break time, kids surged in through the playground doors. I felt bad about the one boy in the school who used a wheelchair. I told the children that we would reward anyone who held doors open or helped each other with books. If anyone was caught fighting on the corridors or even teasing their little brothers or sisters, they would go home that minute. If any invaded a teacher's space, they risked permanent exclusion.

It took almost a fortnight to create and trial the new system for recording serious incidents. At first, the numbers of report slips rose exponentially, just like the graph of a new virus. They peaked at 125 per day or 666 in a week. The emergency calls on the Duty Tutors and Zone Managers also surged. A supply teacher only had to arrive late for a noisy altercation to arise amongst the waiting pupils. But the Zone Manager was at her post and immediately intervened. By the end of January, three of the 10 zones felt secure at all times. The staff in those areas were some of the most assertive in the school. They had quickly adapted their already well-developed ways of managing children.

During the morning briefing at the end of January, I told the staff that there were clear signs that we had begun to "crack the discipline problems". One of the ways forward was to try to harness the good will of the pupils who were starting to change. This meant that we had to learn to forgive. Once sanctions were administered, we had to let go of our frustrations. Labels like "little toe rag" were abrasive and counterproductive. They had no place in Guided Discipline.

Our sanctions were not a licence for revenge, but a way of teaching children how to behave. It should be clear to everyone by now that the most effective ways of shaping pupil behaviour meant the patient reiteration of clear rules and positive reinforcement, not sanctions. We needed to promote good behaviour, give even the worst behaved children fresh opportunities for success and promote a new repertoire of skills through our rewards.

The cleaners provided the best feedback. They reported which of the classroom floors were still clean at the end of the day and which had begun to deteriorate again. In the previous term, there had been £17000 worth of broken windows. In the first two weeks of this term, they only noticed four smashed windowpanes. They were keen on the new approaches, but they had seen disciplinary reforms come and go under the previous Headteacher. What was important for them was that the Leadership Team saw the changes through. "It's early days yet," they teased me.

With Rhiannon's encouragement, some of the pupils had entered and won a regional newspaper competition to host a pop concert by the number one boy band of the time. She announced in Monday briefing that as a reward for the improvement in the children's behaviour, they would be playing a 20-minute set after school on Thursday night. The first 250 pupils to bring 50 commendation slips to her would get tickets. This would boost the credibility of our positive reinforcement scheme and ensure that invitations were restricted to the most sensible pupils in the school. In the event, this worked well. By Thursday, the tickets were "sold out". The pupils were settled. The whole staff turned out to assist and the concert was a great success.

As we reached the end of January, it was clear that many of the pupils were learning to walk on the left, as in our corridor rules, rather than linking arms, running and jostling as they had been doing the previous term. As I had visited the senior lunch hall one day, there had been a lull in the conversation. So, I quietened the hall and told everyone how well they were doing. This was the kind of atmosphere I wanted every day. The school cook had prepared special biscuits iced with the letter Q (for quiet). I asked the lunch supervisors to give these biscuits to the pupils, who were eating sensibly and talking quietly.

Eydon Vale was like a roller coaster ride. A good moment was when the press arrived to take pictures of the concert. However, that same evening Rhiannon was told that the observer from the Office for Standards in Education would be arriving the next day. Christian Dean would be spending three full days a week at the school.

Chapter Six: Secret Friends

By the end of January, far fewer pupils were wandering the corridors. Just as I was carrying out my two o'clock sweep, I spotted Brian Smithson, the Assistant Head, talking to Christian Dean. Quickly introduced, his manner appeared detached, pleasant and non-confrontational. He assured me that he was an independent consultant, not an HMI or an Ofsted Inspector. He had been tasked with reporting to the Secretary of State if Eydon Vale seemed to be sliding out of control. His role was to observe what was happening and write regular reports. I decided to take him at his word and invite his help in evidence gathering.

The first opportunity was at the parents' forum that Rhiannon had called at the end of January. Following Ofsted's initial criticisms of the poor communications between school and the parents, she had instigated a series of monthly open meetings. December's forum had been attended by almost 100 parents. She and Brian Smithson had had to face a barrage of accusations of poor teaching and discipline. On this occasion, the numbers present had fallen slightly, but there was still a buzz in the school hall. The Deputy Director of the Local Authority was slated to appear with the Chair of Trustees, Sir Henry Robinson, Rhiannon and myself. Unfortunately, the Deputy Director had a pressing engagement and Sir Henry was late, so Rhiannon asked me to open the meeting with an overview of our new discipline policy.

So, I summarised the system of rules, rewards and sanctions that the staff had agreed at the start of term. I explained how Mary Stevens of the Local Authority's Behaviour Support Service and I were observing how these were working out in the classroom and on the corridors. "I visit every classroom at least twice a week and am on duty every break and lunchtime. From all I can gather, the two biggest problems for the pupils are noise and bullying."

This seemed to placate many in the audience. There were nods and smiles. However, one parent asked me how I was going to deal with gang-related revenge attacks. "There's no point telling my son to go to his teacher. If the bullies found out that he'd reported them, they'd get their own back after school. If one of his friends went to the Head on his behalf, he, too, would be beaten up."

I replied, "Yes, I agree. The bullies are winning at the moment. The victims are so scared, they daren't open their mouths. I worry that as they grow up, they are going to become just as bad. The violence spreads from bully to the victim and from that victim to another like a virus. We need to find a way of tracing both victim and perpetrator. To stop it spreading, we need to provide immunity to pupils who act as circuit breakers and defy the code of silence. So, we want your help in setting up a new 'secret friend' strategy. I am inviting all the parents of victims to phone me. I just need the pupil's name and class, and I will do the rest.

"I will arrange for a secret friend to look out for them. It will be someone from his or her class who has the same lessons. The secret friend has to be safe in the knowledge that neither the victim nor the bullies will ever find out who they are. He or she won't be a real friend – just a witness. All that we require of secret friends is that they give me a witness statement. They won't sign it with their name, just a number. If the bully had broken the law, the case would be referred to police and they've agreed to accept the number. In all other instances, the matter will be dealt with internally by the Trustees."

Most parents seemed happy, but one or two were unimpressed. There were mutters of "Grass" and "Telltales". One called out, "That's bang out of order. You jist want to turn the kids into a bunch of spies. It'll just be like Germany here, man. Why can't we tell you who the bag 'eds are and you just shot 'em out?"

"I get your point about informants. The East German secret police employed networks of spies to keep an eye on their school or district. They would relay every bit of tittle-tattle to the authorities. No one felt safe. The secret friend has only one other pupil to oversee for a single, time-limited period. If the evidence stands up and the instigator is caught, that's the end of the commitment. Does that answer your question?"

Just as the Chair of Trustees came into the back of the hall, there was an outspoken attack on Ofsted from the parent of one of my gifted Year 11 students. "Five years ago, when Alice started here, it was clear something was seriously wrong with Eydon Vale. Just to give one example: she had hardly any homework. To give another: the marking was patchy. I'm a pilot, Miss Starr. We have anonymous no-blame strategies. If this had been an aircraft, someone would have told the authorities about these issues long before discipline broke down. But because Ofsted is a blame game, nobody said anything. Checks should have been carried out before this plane crash, Miss Starr."

The Chair of Trustees apologised for his lateness and said he would pass on the complaint to Ofsted. He restated the recent history of Eydon Vale and the difficulties that the central government, the local council and the academy trust had had in deciding on its future. He restated his support for the new building and said that, from all he had heard, Eydon Vale had already started to improve. Most of the parents agreed that the school was already much quieter and that the children were working harder. Those with Year 11 children in the higher GCSE sets were delighted with the extra classes.

Sir Henry's intervention undoubtedly affected the mood of the meeting. Much of the parents' dissatisfaction dissipated, though several still wanted someone to blame. Towards the end of the meeting, the mother of one Year 7 pupil said how sad she was that her child's first term was wasted. If only she had known how bad things had been, the boy would have gone to another school, along with her friends' children.

There were also demands from several parents for an official investigation and the apportioning of responsibility between the former Head, Miss Starr and the LEA. Sir Henry said he was not allowed to comment further for legal reasons, but that did not stop the more vocal parents from making allegations against existing and former staff. Much to everyone's embarrassment, one said that Miss Starr's position as the previous head's deputy had been compromised and I should be the next Headteacher. As the meeting concluded, one of the parents came up to me and gave me a kiss. "How are you doing?" she said. "I'm Alice Lawton's mother."

"I remember. You interviewed me."

"Alice says your lessons are 'awesome'. She told me that you emailed one of her essays back, marked and corrected, at 5:30 in the morning. You gave her Grade 9. She could not believe it. Please don't go breaking their hearts."

Next morning, I had a phone call from Mr Appleby, the father of a Year 7 boy called Nicholas. Every day since he started at Eydon Vale, the same Year 11 student had been stealing his dinner money from him. It had been torture, not knowing if he would be hit or how badly he would be hurt every lunchtime. It had gone on for so long, that Nicholas's father had felt powerless.

Having worked out which boys had the same lessons as Nicholas, I asked his form tutor for advice about which of them would be best as a secret friend. Two of them were ruled out as everyone knew they were buddies of Nicholas. The third readily assented, safe in the knowledge that no one would ever guess he had been an informant. Anthony Plimpton trailed around after Nicholas during the next day's lunch break, and it was not long before he observed the bully in the act.

Anthony immediately reported to my office as agreed and wrote a statement, signing it with the number. I then sent for the boy who had carried out the bullying: Phil Jimson. Asked if he minded turning out his pockets and confronted with the evidence of the secret friend, Phil admitted the truth and wrote his confession.

"Why did you do it?" I asked.

"It happened to me when I started here, and no one seemed bothered," Phil replied.

It had been agreed by the staff that if pupils broke the law, we should inform the police. Because Eydon Vale had been categorised as a "turbulent school", the Home Office had asked the local constabulary to prioritise our needs. So, when Rhiannon Starr contacted the local police, there was an immediate response. By 1:30 that afternoon, Phil and Mrs Jimson were in the police station. He was charged with demanding money with menaces and suspended from school. His mother was asked to bring him into school on his return for a formal meeting with the Governors' disciplinary sub-committee. The news quickly spread around the school. No one knew who the informer was. This sense of uncertainty had an immediate and dramatic effect on the statistical data we had just begun to gather. No one knew which bully would be our next victim.

One of the suggestions made in our Action Plan was that there would be half-termly sampling of exercise books, coursework and artefacts in to monitor homework and marking. According to the plan we had agreed for the division of responsibilities, this was Rhiannon's area, so after the parents' meeting, she decided to make an immediate start on this. I suggested an approach I had instigated at Rectory Road, based on the letters of the alphabet.

We agreed that in this instance we would collect the work of all pupils, whose surnames begin with the letter O. All the European Commission evidence suggested that Roma children and travellers of Irish heritage were the two ethnic groups most likely to underachieve. So, this was a discreet way of monitoring the latter. This gave us a small but reasonably sized sample, which included boys and girls from the entire ability range. Christian Dean was only too happy to join us.

Some staff "forgot" to send us their pupils' books, but even so, it was clear from the marking audit that most of the staff were starting to give more homework. True, some tasks were make-work and took only 10 minutes for the children to complete, but others would have taken three hours. Most of the pupils in this sample appeared to be doing between two hours a week and six.

Many staff were also starting to give feedback on effort. A few had begun engaging in a dialogue with students. Their comments included questions to which some pupils were responding. The best remarks were clear, informative and affirmative and they showed pupils how to improve their attainment. However, a significant proportion of the books had no marks at all. One Maths teacher had simply ticked all the sums in the book, right or wrong. Others were just commenting on the need to put the date and underline headings. And there was no evidence that Heads of Department were monitoring assessments within their team groups.

After we had looked at the books, we convened a focus group of the pupils concerned. They said that they had done more homework in the last month than ever at the school and were very positive about this. They also appreciated the teachers' use of praise and commendations. When we asked them to estimate how many of the staff were teaching them well enough, they agreed that three-quarters of the staff were "doing OK". Our own analysis of the books and homework tasks bore this out; approximately 70% of the staff seemed to be doing an adequate job and we had four excellent teachers.

These pupils also said that a quarter of the teachers were still "too soft". When I asked them to give concrete examples of what they meant by "too soft", one Year 9 pupil replied. "Take Rule Four: no calling out. All the teachers insist on this when you come in the classroom, Sir, and most continue when you've left. You have to put up your hand and wait quietly. But others turn a blind eye. Kids in those lessons were still being allowed to shout out the answers. This can be a major distraction. They make self-conscious girls like me feel excluded."

During our discussion, the focus group reported that the introduction of secret friends had virtually extinguished physical bullying. "The first day I was here, someone slashed me in a Maths lesson," Elroy Samson, one of the few mixed-race boys at Eydon Vale, told us. "There was a gang that used to scissor a razor blade in half and super glue the blades either side of a school ruler. They were so sharp; I didn't notice the cut until the blood ran down my arm. When I got to the hospital, the A&E nurse could not give me stitches because it was a double wound. My mum made a complaint about racism in the school, but the old Head did not even reply. There was no real investigation. There was no immunity for the witnesses. I still have the scars."

Christian Dean joined in our discussion with the children and evidently enjoyed it. He told us he was impressed by the start that we had made. It was clear to him, too, that three-quarters of the classes were quieter and that the pupils particularly appreciated the teachers' use of praise and commendations. However, he dropped a broad hint that if we had failed to eliminate dangerous behaviour such as the slashing Elroy described, Eydon Vale would be bulldozed before August.

The Thursday that marked the end of that first month happened to be both the most unsettled afternoon of the new term *and* the date of the next Governors' meeting. Every break, scuffles would surface in the playground, but there was one particularly violent fight that lunchtime. A substantial amount of vandalism had also occurred in the toilets. During the last lesson of the day, I was teaching my bottom set Year 9s and the three Heads of Year, whose priority should have been to patrol the corridors, were held up in a child protection meeting. Four girls were on the loose, defying the support staff. There were three fights in separate classrooms. Christian Dean witnessed one of these and when I saw him after school, he discreetly reminded me of the closure deadline.

At the Governors' meeting later that evening, Rhiannon gave a dispassionate and credible report. Despite the success of our training programme and the introduction of our new Discipline Policy, we were still having "bad moments". This had been our worst afternoon since Christmas. We still had no bursar, and when Rhiannon's PA, Edwina Brown distributed the figures for our end of year financial projection, these indicated a probable overspend of £145 000.

At this point, the Academy Trust's Treasurer interjected. She had also inspected the figures. She announced that Edwina's estimates gravely under-estimated the problem. Not only were her present figures out by 130%: she had miscalculated the projected bill for supply staff. By the end of the financial year, this shortfall would probably top a third of a million pounds.

The new Chair of Governors, Jacob Hornsby, took this comment very calmly. He wound up the meeting by telling Rhiannon how important it was that everyone held their nerve. We would have our bad days. The key thing was whether the pupils were working harder and settling down. He felt confident that the children knew that Eydon Vale was now becoming a safer school and he formally assured her of the Governors' support.

He did not explain his grounds for such optimism at the time. What had happened was that he had taken the lead in interviewing the pupils from Eydon Vale who had applied for places at his Sixth Form College. They had told him about the extra homework and classes. It was clear to him these pupils were making rapid progress. Their gossip about a sea change in behaviour had been enough to assure him we were "on the right track".

Chapter Seven: Half Term Break

Rhiannon was called out of school at least twice a week, so I was often left to conduct the morning staff briefings. So, the day after the Governors' Meeting, I had to announce that we had their support. My latest observations indicated that many colleagues were now sufficiently relaxed to start teaching well. The number of serious incidents was falling but still high. One of the Year 9 boys had been caught urinating in a stairwell. However, there was a more significant issue: how to win over the silent majority. The pupils had to make up their minds about whose side they were on: the adults' or the troublemakers'.

When Rhiannon returned from that morning's conference, she reported that the immediate crisis was over. The threat of immediate closure had been lifted and the Chair of Trustees had reiterated his confidence in the Senior Management Team. Rhiannon had been permitted to advertise three of the Heads of Departments' posts on that basis. The Trust was confident that it could enable Rhiannon to ease the least competent teachers out of their posts quickly, without causing further staffing difficulties.

When I told her about my idea for a Roll of Honour Evening, she was extremely receptive. I had seen this in operation when lecturing in Canada. Schools all over North America will put the names of the most gifted academically, the sporting stars, the most talented musicians and actors and those who demonstrate good citizenship on the "Dean's list" and awarded an "Honor Roll" certificate.

Even though the time for preparation was short, Rhiannon decided to hold the first award ceremony in the first week back to school after half term. She asked the Heads of Year to nominate about 20 children from each Year Group. These were generally the pupils with the highest number of Commendations for hard work in class and for putting extra effort into their homework. We also invited the Year 7 Boys' and Girls' Football Teams, as they had come top of their Leagues. No pupil would be allowed to come without a parent and because of space restrictions, we could only allow one parent per pupil.

Rhiannon and I told each of the assemblies that the names of the pupils we invited would be put on the Eydon Vale Roll of Honour. Their photos would be displayed in the case at the front of the school. They would get a certificate and, most importantly, a pass to the new Tuck Shop. That was what stirred interest. Virtually every system within Eydon Vale had been broken at the New Year. Even the wheels on the minibus were flat! The only exceptions were the sporting facilities and food. By chance, we had the services of a first-rate chef and excellent pastry cook.

Why were we doing this? The evening was designed to announce the inauguration of a new vision. After the half-term break, Eydon Vale would rise from the ashes again. We believed that if this vision were to be turned into reality, we would need the active support of more and more pupils and parents. There would be a second Roll of Honour evening at the start of the Summer Term and a third by that half term.

A couple of days later, Rhiannon came to my office in the school foyer. I thought she was going to tell me about her latest success in organising speakers. But what she said was that I was suspended. I had been accused of assaulting a Year 11 pupil called Ian. As I was standing by the double doors that morning, ushering the last pupils into school at the end of our mid-morning break, I noticed that Ian had a nasty red weal on the back of his neck. I thought at first that this might have been caused by scabies. My death stare had made him feel uncomfortable and he muttered a casual insult at me: "Baldy headed ding!"

He ignored my instruction to stop. He simply carried on down the corridor. I told him to stop again but to no avail. His attitude was openly defiant. There were some new security doors at the end of this section of the corridor. Connor, the caretaker, was standing by them and I told him to shut the doors to stop the boys going through them. As Ian paused, I asked his name. He refused to look at me and ignored my direction. One of the younger pupils, passing in the opposite direction, bravely told me what it was. I followed Ian to our Reception Base for the pupils who had committed serious breaches of the Disciplinary Code. Each time he went through the security doors, he tried to slam them against me, but the safety springs would not allow this.

Rhiannon had been out at yet another meeting and had left me in charge for the morning. I told Veronica Stonehouse, the Manager of the Reception Base, what had happened and asked her to contact his carers. When Veronica asked Ian where the scratches on his neck came from, his friend Matthew said, "Mr Shaw grabbed him". This was a malicious fabrication. Ian himself shrugged his shoulders. When Veronica looked at the neck, it did appear to her to be grazed, but the marks did not seem recent. She asked him again what had happened, and he replied, "Mr Shaw grabbed me."

Veronica warned him how careful he needed to be about making serious accusations. Ian continued to be belligerent and truanted from the Reception Base just before lunch. At lunchtime, Veronica told me about his complex home situation and how he had run off before the foster carer had had a chance to chance to drive in. I asked her to write a brief report about what she had seen of the incident and report his disappearance to an Education Social Worker and the police.

The foster carer arrived shortly afterwards, and I interviewed him with Veronica. The man admitted that Ian had accused him of making the scratches before school that morning. He obligingly made a written report, which he then signed. I asked him to bring Ian into school the next morning, telephone the boy's social worker and make a mutually convenient appointment the next morning.

When Rhiannon saw the reports of the incidents from Veronica, Connor the caretaker, the foster carer and me, her initial reaction was to remove me from the school. She was happy to let the police and social services find out the truth in their own time. I told her quite bluntly that according to the DfE's latest guidelines, she did not have to send me home that afternoon. If the balance of probabilities was that these allegations were baseless, then she was permitted to carry out her own investigation first. She ought at least to see the two boys who were with Ian in the Reception Base before making up her mind. She agreed to review the official guidance on the internet and read the statements but told me to stay in my office while she did so.

Given the direction from the Home Office to prioritise Eydon Vale, the police quickly caught up with Ian. They indicated that as the pupil himself did not wish to bring charges, they could proceed no further. A multi-agency meeting was called that evening, which concluded that there were no grounds for action against Ian or me. Rhiannon immediately texted me with their conclusion, but I barely dozed that night.

For the first two terms at Eydon Vale, I worked an 18-hour day and often slept just three hours a night. Just as when I was a university lecturer, I would often be out of bed by five o'clock putting the final touches to the next day's teaching. At least, there was a break during university vacations. Over that first February half-term holiday at Eydon Vale, the staff ran four days of additional classes for the targeted pupils in Year 11. We knew that if all the targeted children improved their grades in ICT, Maths, English and Science, this would transform the school's exam statistics. Hard evidence like this was just what Ofsted would need before taking Eydon Vale out of special measures.

The first of the extra sessions was to be in English. All those in the Year 11 top set had been invited together with a further ten pupils from the second stream. Among them were Pete Sangster and three members of his crew. They were all to revise key passages from their set nineteenth-century novel: Jane Eyre.

All my class had all been attending regular Monday night and Saturday morning classes. The pupils had also been asked for six hours of homework per week. In the previous half term, they had looked at the poetry anthology and reread Romeo and Juliet. During this period, there had been a rapid improvement in reading accuracy and comprehension, although written English still lacked precision and fluency. Nevertheless, by the February half term, the number of targeted students who were attaining the highest three levels had quadrupled since after Christmas.

The first topic to address that morning was Jane's experience of Lowood School. He asked the pupils to turn to the scene where Jane comes face to face with Mr Brocklehurst, its tyrannical owner.

"Passages like this are likely to feature in the new style GCSE English Literature paper. What I want you to do is pick out keywords and phrases just like you would for a poem or a Shakespeare speech. Then make notes in the margin about their literal meaning and wider connotations; Jane's feelings as well as those it evokes in you; the rhetorical devices Brontë is employing and their implications for structure and context. Context is crucial: you have to show the examiners how well you know the novel. I will give you ten minutes."

Several of the pupils had arrived without breakfast, and as they were reading, they wolfed down the fruit and croissants I had provided. Pete Sangster had called out, "Please sir, I want some more", but the rest of the pupils shushed him.

In the discussion that followed, Elroy Samson led the way. He focused on Charlotte Brontë's image of Brocklehurst as "the black marble clergyman". As he explained, "In those colonial times, when British middle-class families had got rich from the fortunes that the Government gave them in reparation for freeing their Afro-Caribbean slaves, blackness had particular connotations. Their residual guilt was projected on to black people. There was no such thing as political correctness in those days."

There were sniggers from Peter, but a death stare silenced him. "Excellent start, Elroy. Does anyone else want to look at the layers of meaning that Elroy is alluding to?"

Gillian Newsome put up her hand. She may not have Elroy's originality, but she had always listened carefully to everything said in class. She was determined to bring the connotations of ethnicity to which Elroy had been alluding into focus. "You can see the same sort of thing in Charlotte Brontë's representation of Bertha, the Creole woman hidden away in Rochester's attic. She's characterised as 'a wild animal' and 'a clothed hyena'. For contemporary readers, the colour black would have held associations with cruelty and horror."

Following Gillian's lead and my praise, many other pupils in the group put up their hands. One of Peter's crew noted the implicit comparison between Brocklehurst and the "white stone" image that Charlotte sees in St John Rivers.

"Excellent: you are sticking closely to the words that Brontë uses. So, let me put the question back to you. What do Brontë's words tell us about these two men?" asked the Head.

"They are both clergymen and both hard-hearted," replied the pupil, as I threw him a chocolate bar.

Not to be outshone by one of his acolytes, Pete Sangster now added his thoughts. He argued, "At least St John puts his money where his mouth is. We might have lots of criticisms of his behaviour, but he was no hypocrite. St John rescued Jane when she was lost and starving on the moors. He encouraged her to set up a school for the poor. He was prepared to sacrifice his health and career to spread the gospel in India. But what makes Brocklehurst so objectionable is his sanctimony."

"If you use long words like that in the exam, the markers will be asking themselves, 'Which school does this one go to? Harrow or Eton?' Chocolate for you, too!"

Alice Lawton, the daughter of the parent governor and the pilot, pointed out that Charlotte Brontë used clothes to symbolise moral values. "Jane is nearly always dressed in 'Quaker grey' to show her integrity. In this extract, there is a contrast between the meagre 'brown uniforms' that Brocklehurst bought for the pupils and 'the spread of shot orange and purple silk pelisses and a cloud of silvery plumage' in which he dressed his daughters. All these colours form a background to Jane and Brocklehurst as he singled her out for punishment. In getting Jane to stand on the stool, Charlotte Brontë wants us to see the disparity. He is not just cruel: as Pete says, he is a hypocrite. As for Jane: she's so angry with the world, she is too honest. She lets herself become a martyr for the truth."

Finally, the group began to focus on the sanctions Brocklehurst imposed. "What links Victorian clergymen like Brocklehurst and St John is the way they set out to mortify the flesh," said Ming Lee. "This repels the orphan Jane. Right from the start she instinctively seeks out love. She sees red Mrs Reed's cruelty, as Alice implies. It is a red room she's sent to, hence the projection which Elroy was explaining. The only member of staff at Lowood to win Jane over is Miss Temple. She teaches her how to govern her temper. But she only succeeded through love and praise."

"And better food," added Pete cockily.

"Quite right. Miss Temple gives the girls bread and cheese when the porridge was burnt. You make the analysis of nineteenth-century literature sound like a piece of cake, Peter."

The discussion involved over 30 of those present. Afterwards, there was a PowerPoint which summarised many of the points that I thought the examiners would be seeking. The group then wrote a timed essay. This pattern of discussion, presentation and essay was repeated after the mid-morning break.

As they left for home at the end of the morning, a girl called Mairead O'Connell handed over a note excusing herself from the following Monday's after school lesson. She had an ophthalmologist's appointment.

"New glasses?" I smiled.

"I have been having dizzy spells for the three weeks," she replied. "I tell my mum that you're teaching us how to use our brains at last, but she's worried..."

"That I'm giving you too much homework... Tell me how you get on, would you? And try to relax over the weekend."

The atmosphere that morning had been exhilarating. The tone of the arguments was rigorous and without rancour. The class had begun to explore much more challenging work patterns. They wrote with high levels of concentration and in absolute silence. By the Thursday of the half-term break, when everyone was tired and irritable, Pete directed a racist remark at Elroy, and they squared up.

Peter's crew had echoed his remark, deliberately taunting Erol. Pete struck the first blow, which Elroy successfully evaded. Elroy had a longer reach and was faster on his feet. A jab from Elroy had then broken Peter's nose. The exchange of blows had only lasted a few moments. By the time the Maths staff arrived, Peter's school shirt was covered in blood. The fight was over.

As Miss Starr drove into the staff car park, a police car and an ambulance were already standing outside Eydon Vale. There was little doubt in the constables' minds that both Pete and Elroy were at fault. They thought that it might be better if the school dealt with the incident internally. Miss Starr was adamant that Elroy had committed actual bodily harm, though. Peter's parents would need to see that justice would be done. She would be excluding Elroy pending police action. In the event, both lads were cautioned. Elroy only missed a couple of days' school, though his name was taken off the Roll of Honour.

For the awards evening, the caretakers laid out the hall chairs in a double ellipse. The pupils were to sit in the inner ring with their parent behind them, so the parents could take photos as they returned to their seats. The Head's PA wrote all the invitations and organised flowers for the table. The school's Community Outreach Worker designed the Certificates, invited a local pop star and helped the caretakers with the overall design of the hall.

The parents and pupils began to arrive at about 5.40 and were seated by their Heads of Year in alphabetical order. The guest speakers were greeted at the front door by Laura. I expected that less than 40 of the 125 pupils invited would come, but in the event, 120 turned up with a parent. At 6.10, the pupils and their parents were asked to stand for entry of the speakers. The evening opened with a brief welcome from Rhiannon. Sir Henry then gave a powerful oration, balancing the threats to the school's continued existence with the progress made so far.

Sir Henry called on me to outline the roles of rewards, recognition and reinforcement in Guided Discipline. I compared what was happening to a vital episode in the history of science. In the first public demonstration of electromagnetism at the Royal Institution, Michael Faraday had placed compasses underneath a copper wire, thrown a switch and made all the needles swing into a mysterious new pattern. We wanted to establish new norms of behaviour and learning.

There was a feeling of joy in the Hall and several parents wept. It felt as if everyone present was willing us to succeed. Jacob Hornsby, the Chair of the new Governing Body, presented the Roll of Honour Certificates. In his speech of congratulations, he said this simple ceremony was the best awards evening he had ever attended because it meant so much to the participants. He encouraged the children to be proud of their achievements. No one must ever feel ashamed of doing well at school.

In his view, Eydon Vale had just begun to turn a corner and the children and parents in front of him had had a vital part to play in that process. Jacob's remarks were extremely timely. His interviews of our Year 11 pupils had helped him put his finger on the pulse of the school and he grasped that we were embarked on the process of recovery. He and Rhiannon then presented the pupils with their certificates and entry passes for the Tuck Shop.

After the pop singer had sung the song that had helped him win Britain's Got Talent, Rhiannon wound up the evening with a vote of thanks. As they gathered around the tea tables, parents and pupils alike seemed bewildered by their achievements.

Chapter Eight: Vertigo

The Roll of Honour Evening had several unforeseen consequences. One of these was to prompt a fresh willingness among the younger staff to take risks. The role played by Rowena Cross, the school's only full-time RE teacher, was crucial. Her Master's was in the Study of Adolescent Spiritual Experiences, but after six months as a teacher, she was still unsure if spirituality could ever be taught.

Most of her problems stemmed from pupils who had learned bad habits rather than those with profound psychological problems. One morning Patrick Wadsworth, a bubbly Year 8 boy with mild literacy difficulties, deliberately spat in her mug when her back was turned, then watched her drink her coffee. That night Patrick discovered that his grandfather had just died of tuberculosis.

Rowena lived at home, and her parents put a lot of pressure on her to leave teaching. She needed her whole sick leave to get her bearings. Her dark nights of the soul prompted her to rethink her lesson plans in line with her academic interests. At her return to work interview, she told me, "I'm going to find new ways of channelling her pupils' spiritual experiences."

For her first lesson back, she asked Patrick's class what came into their heads when she used the word "God". At first, they baulked. Everyone knew what a risk she was taking. This topic was even more taboo than sex, especially if it was to be led by such an innocent. They all stared at her blankly and she held the silence.

Perhaps they pitied her after her health scare. Eventually, one boy said he pictured God as an old man with a beard, sitting on his throne. Another argued that since we all had a conscience, it had to come from someone or something. Just as I slipped into the room, Jo Johnson, a fanciful girl with white hair and fair skin, put up her hand. "Miss, I had a dream last night." She hesitated in case one of Patrick's friends cracked a joke, but none did. For once, they were all attention. "I was in New York on a tightrope. It was stretched between the Twin Towers. I felt dizzy but did not fall off. That feeling of vertigo woke me up.

"I have had that unstable feeling a couple of times before. It's like fear, but I am not afraid. I have not got anything to be frightened of. Everything is fine at home and school's more bearable. Until now, I have tried to forget the feeling. But now I'm beginning to think it's something deep: a force to be respected. God's in this sense of losing your balance. If you let it overpower you, you could come crashing down. But without that sense of vertigo, would you have a soul?"

Noha, a recently arrived Somalian refugee, was next in accepting Rowena's challenge. Before she came to England, she had won medals for middle distance. "When I am running," she said, "God is there. God is not coming first or winning a medal or getting on the Roll of Honour. God is my secret, my anger and my freedom. Nothing else matters when I hit my stride. I feel free to my soul."

There was a catch in Rowena's voice as she said, "Does anyone else have anything to say?"

Then Patrick apologised. "What I did to you, Miss, made me wonder what I'm really like." Amends had been made; good order restored. For Noha and her class, this was a turning point. There was a short-lived, new competition: who could do the most homework.

What made the lesson doubly exciting was the way individual children were daring to challenge the conventional thinking of their classmates. Jo Johnson revelation of her vertigo was exposing her emotional vulnerability and allowing her to be more open in her thinking. One or two of the other staff had been mentioning similar examples of open debate. Their pupils had been feeling safe enough to disagree with their friends, too. The trauma of all the previous months had blunted the children's originality and reinforced conformity, but they might just be moving on at last.

Later that day, when I was visiting Kate Bullamore's Technology class, she also mentioned this feeling of vertigo. She joked that her blood pressure probably needed checking. But she also said that the balance was shifting in the school. "It's almost as if the ground is shifting under our feet. The troublemakers are losing. This school is not their territory so much. The rest of the children are starting to trust us once more. It's good, but it gives me a dizzy feeling."

There was something strange going on. There was no way Kate could have heard about Rowena's RE class, yet she was experiencing something very similar to Jo Johnson. The confidence that should attend an effective and experienced teacher like Kate could evaporate at a moment's notice. The ethos was shifting, yet the reforms we were putting in place were still so deeply fragile. Nothing was safe or secure. Some experienced this sense of liminality as positive, others as disturbing.

The Celebration of Achievement Evening also attracted the attention of the local MP. Tom Shelton was a high-ranking cabinet minister. He had arrived one morning with his police escort and bodyguard for an unscheduled private inspection. I asked Rhiannon's PA to get her back from her out of school meeting, whilst I gave him a conducted tour.

As we went around the school, Tom cross-questioned me about our intake. He found our statistics on local crime, child homelessness and deprivation sobering. Of the 12599 parishes in England, Eydon Vale had one of the 200 highest rates of child poverty. 35% of the local children were entitled to Free School Meals, while slightly fewer came from dislocated families. He was particularly interested in the effect we were having on the hopes and achievements of our white working-class boys. "Their needs have slipped to the bottom of the in-tray."

When Rhiannon arrived, Tom deliberately circled her, so that she could not see me. He seemed to square up to her and look into her eyes. He grilled her about Guided Discipline and asked her point-blank how sure she was that *she* could re-establish good order at the school. As I escorted him from the building, he accepted an invitation to the next Roll of Honour evening.

Tom Shelton took a personal interest in Eydon Vale, despite a crushing ministerial workload. He visited the school three times during that year. At the ceremony, he spoke about his beginnings and how important his education had had in helping him overcome a poor start in life as the child of a single mother, raised on benefits.

A couple of weeks after half term, I arranged a trip to the local theatre as a reward for the Year 11s who had come into school in the holidays. An acclaimed, touring production of Jane Eyre was playing. Many in the top set English class knew what to expect from a visit to the theatre. They had been to "The Grand" for pantomimes or musicals. They were determined to have a good night out and had all dressed appropriately. Two girls had ordered a table at an Italian restaurant beforehand. Others arrived in taxis. Two got out of their sickbeds. One even limped in on crutches and the theatre staff put her and her friend in a box.

The director was keen to involve local pupils in theatre workshops whenever the company put on a show, so on the following afternoon, two actors came into school. The taxi driver who brought them had joked that this was such a rough school, they should have brought baseball bats. They took the pupils through a series of actors' exercises and helped the class to talk through issues of reality and appearance in Jane Eyre. The pupils' questions showed a high degree of understanding. In the last half-hour, as the rest of the school was packing up, groups of pupils improvised scenes from the novel themselves. Outside the doors, there was a tremendous racket but the actors kept their nerve and the pupils their concentration.

At the end of the first week back, we opened the tuck shop to the pupils who were on our Roll of Honour. The Governors upheld the first permanent exclusion that Eydon Vale had made in three or four years. And after two days of interviews, Rhiannon had appointed Heads of Department to fill the vacancies in Maths, ICT and Science. Sir Henry had also spent a huge amount of time fruitlessly persuading the other Heads in our Academy Trust to "lend" us experienced, dynamic teachers.

All too predictably, the Headteachers worried that their schools might be weakened, too. There was no compulsion for any to offer help and no pressure on their teachers to volunteer. There was not even any extra government money to sweeten the pill. So, in the event, only one volunteered, a talented but unhappy Modern Linguist.

As she joined the school, one of the Art teachers dropped out. Gillian had missed the initial training in Guided Discipline while on long-term sick leave due to stress and was barely coping. I offered to role-play a mini-lesson to demonstrate the agreed procedures. Gillian then gave a wonderful lesson with a difficult Year 9 group. She had been full of presence and very assertive. However, the effort had been too much for her and she resigned.

Some of the staff had started joining the Heads of Year and me during their non-contact time as we toured the building, scouting for the last of the internal truants. As a result of all our endeavours, there had been even fewer pupils wandering the corridors. For the remnant, we formalised our policy, putting each of them in front of Governors and the Education Social Worker for truancy.

As the pupils' attitude appeared to improve, the staff thought they could drop their guard. The observations of Mary Stevens from the LEA's

Behaviour Support Service and the independent consultant Christian Dean bore out my own. Rule Four was being forgotten: "When you need attention, raise your hand and wait silently". The tally of praise, rewards and reinforcement was dropping, too.

One morning just before the end of term, Rhiannon came back from one of her meetings with the news that we were to expect a series of mini-inspections. Mary, Christian and I persuaded her that the key issue was pupil talk. There was too much idle chat and too much calling out in lessons. Even where the pupils were relatively quiet, they were still fidgety and restless. The other side of the coin was that when pupils joined in the discussion, they often lacked the confidence to speak at length. They found difficulty in explaining their ideas with the appropriate, technical vocabulary. They had forgotten the rhythms of conventional whole-class conversation.

During the next in-service training evening, I explained to the staff that we all had a role in helping our pupils find a way out of the vicious cycle, whichever subject we were teaching. The most effective way for any of us to learn anything was to listen to the teacher. But we also needed to listen to our peers; to answer the teacher's questions, and to make our own comments. Most of us only understand what we think when we hear ourselves saying it!

The staff then carried out some role play on questioning strategies. By the end of the evening, it was clear that we all needed to be much more consistent about the kind of talking we would and would not accept. We should always meet positive contributions with praise and reinforcement. Infringements of our boundaries should be challenged with reminders about listening to staff and putting hands up. There should be sanctions for interruptions and quiet time for independent work every lesson.

I told the staff that we had already travelled a long way over the previous half term in our control of the pupils' behaviour. "Guided Discipline is more than rules, rewards and sanctions. What it also demands is a determination to keep moving forwards. To adopt the military analogy that Brian Jameson had made in his inaugural address: if we stayed in our foxholes, we would be defeated. Just like frontline infantry, we had to keep advancing. Ofsted would be unforgiving if we just dictated lesson notes, gave out worksheets, or let the pupils call out in an undisciplined manner. We also needed to encourage the use of more exact words, keywords, technical vocabulary; and practice clarifying and explaining."

This re-launch of Guided Discipline and the opening of the Tuck Shop improved staff morale and calmed the children. Despite this, there were still anarchic episodes. The school was recovering from something akin to a potentially lethal virus. Most of the time, the temperature was close to normal, but every once in a while, it would shoot up again. Just when these "spikes" occurred was almost impossible to predict. On some days, the school building would be quiet for periods of half an hour or more, only to be disrupted by a single, freakish incident, which could, in turn, spark off a larger scale, group disturbance.

One day, a Year 7 pupil was injured by someone throwing a coin across the playground. His face was bleeding and an ambulance had had to be called. The ambulance crew took the child out, just as the bell rang for the end of lunch. Instead of going straight to lessons, a huge crowd congregated in the foyer. It reminded Rhiannon of the "rubbernecks", stopping their cars at a motorway accident. Three minutes later, the crowd had dispersed, and the children were back at work. But they had shown, once again, this fascination that disorder still held for them.

When I mentioned this temperature spike analogy to Christian Dean, he suggested that over the next couple of weeks Brian Smithson and I should try to predict the pattern of behaviour for the next day, then see what happened. Our prognostications were quite different and both wrong. Brian was too pessimistic. He thought there would be more fights than transpired. And I was caught out by a new craze.

This new vogue was the throwing of plastic sandwich bags filled with liquid. This was not enough for George Pearson, a Year 8 pupil. He filled his bait bag with urine and chucked it into a queue outside the toilets. Several pupils and a lunchtime supervisor were splashed. At first, we were unable to locate a single witness. The next day he repeated the trick, drenching one of the few African pupils at Eydon Vale. On his way back into the loos, George slipped and cut his lip on a basin. He tried to blame Elroy Samson for his injury, but two of the Year 8s on our Honour Roll reported the incident.

George was given a lengthy fixed term exclusion. Interestingly, Elroy did not deny George's accusations, even after he had been exonerated. I failed to understand why until the next term when I heard the full story of his father's suicide in a police cell. Elroy was to carry around a sense of guilt all the time I knew him. He would take the blame for incidents that had nothing to do with him.

Now that the school was becoming calmer, the behaviour of individual pupils with marked psychological problems was becoming more conspicuous. Up to this point, the general behaviour in the school had been so disorderly that their difficulties had been masked. Now, their behaviour was beginning to stand out. Jack Andrews, a high-flier in my Year 11 set, had sudden panics and temper tantrums that reminded me of the children in our special unit for children with Asperger's at Rectory Road.

George Pearson's attitudes were shared by a subculture within the school, on the other hand. When George was first questioned about throwing the bag of urine, he vehemently denied it. Confronted by our witness statements, his response was a shrug. His attitude seemed to be: "Can't you see it was just a joke?"

The interplay of pupils like Jack, George, Elroy and Pete Sangster was dizzyingly complex. We could tabulate the numbers of staff Cause for Concern reports and analyse probabilities but could not predict our worst moments. At this stage, the only way we could make sense of individual behaviour was through patient, post-hoc narratives.

This seemed to be borne out later in the year. Some Sheffield University researchers were hired by the Home Office to carry out semi-structured interviews in the school. The children told them that they found the story of the school's recovery endlessly fascinating. Every night they would go home and tell their parents about the latest episode or try to make sense of it with their friends.

The first of the "mini-inspections" that Rhiannon had told us to expect was carried out by Dick Twinings, the freelance consultant used by the DfES on key projects, who had first visited Eydon Vale at its worst moment in the previous November. As he stood in the foyer picking up the mood of the school, a broad smile spread across his features. He spent most of his time with Rhiannon and Sir Henry, though he also popped into a couple of lessons.

The children knew something was up. With the exceptions of six pupils with high levels of psychological disturbance, they responded very positively. Dick's visit had been arranged by the DfES to determine the viability of the school and to examine all the alternatives, should it be closed. As he left, a group of French schoolchildren happened to arrive at the school as part of a school exchange. Chatting to their teacher, who had visited the school in previous years, Dick was overheard to say that Eydon Vale now appeared to be *"Presque normale"*.

Chapter Nine: The Runner

Noha Malek came from a tiny group of Somalian refugee families who had been sent to Holmesside under the Government's dispersal policy. Her father had left Africa the previous year for a job as a consultant at the university hospital. He and his wife had separated, though, and Noha now lived with her mother in wretched Local Authority accommodation. Noha had missed a lot of her education because of the civil war and when she started at Eydon Vale, her ability to read and write English was rudimentary.

One of her neighbours happened to be a teacher. He was a Syrian refugee called Dr Adam Awad. He had previously been the Vice Principal of an international school. Barred from paid post-doctoral research on a new academic project, he volunteered to teach a small group of pupils to read and write in English. He and Noha were neighbours and they continued with one-to-one tutorials in the Christmas holidays under her mother's supervision. By the time of the first Parents' Forum I attended, though, she was still making slow progress with her basic phonics. The lessons only began to pick up when Adam decided they should compose a graphic novel together. It was to be based the novel on the life of a refugee with a background just like Noha's.

The novel's title was to be 'The Runner', This was the nickname that the British press had given her maternal grandfather, Kip, when he had won an Olympic marathon. Noha was a talented runner too. She had won medals back in Somalia in middle distance races. When Kylie Lawrence, Eydon Vale's Head of PE, found out, she gave her trials, Her times at for 1500 metres and 5k were good even by national standards. When Kylie heard that places might still be available at this year's Young Olympians Easter Training Course, she asked me to research sponsorship.

When I heard about the literacy lessons, I sent a message to Adam asking him if he would like to volunteer as a teaching assistant. This might well help his prospects in getting asylum status and paid work. After all the stories Noha must have told him, Adam could have had no illusions about Eydon Vale. He knew about the deliberate smashing of fire alarms; the food filched from the dinner counters; dope smoked at break times and the chemicals stolen from the labs. Adam had studied Fine Arts at

Oxford, and his PhD thesis had been on Sicilian Mosaics. The Art Department needed help and he was delighted to accept Rhiannon's offer of an interview.

As he told Rhiannon, Elizabeth Oliphant (the Head of Art) and me, many aspects of life in modern England shocked him. Among the drawings he had sketched for Noha's novel, there were asylum seekers who had had their doors painted red. In others, he pictured them at food banks, with red armbands. "England used to be more hospitable. It is not as welcoming as it used to be when I was a student here. It's a hostile environment, now."

Now and again, the inner Deputy that Adam thought he had left behind in Syria would come out and startle the pupils. One day, towards the end of the Easter Term, Elizabeth arrived late for an afternoon lesson. The art room door was locked and the Year 8s she was meant to be teaching were milling about. Forgetting that he was only an unpaid Art Assistant, he told them to wait quietly. To his surprise, they immediately fell into line.

Mrs Oliphant shared his enthusiasm for Noha. She gave Noha lots of merits and promised to phone her mother at home. "She has drawn a wonderful picture of a girl running through the streets. I loved her use of light. It is the bright light of Africa. It is so good, I want to put it in for an exhibition at the Town Hall," she gushed. "I think Noha is talented enough to get into Art College when she leaves school. She just needs to get good passes in her GCSE English and Maths."

Rhiannon had made a rule that the school corridors should be clear of children during the midday break. Hardly anyone was allowed a pass. Forthright but charming, Adam told her that the gap between the most and least able was unacceptable. He was appalled to find how few of the pupils at Eydon Vale had been taught grammar and how severely this affected the less able. They did not know the parts of speech or how to parse a sentence. A catch-up class would allow him to focus on these underachievers and bring their writing up to a reasonable standard. Rhiannon agreed and offered to get special passes printed for Noha and a couple of her classmates.

According to Noha's novel, there were sounds of a fight outside the Art Room door one lunchtime. When Adam opened it, Noha could see a Year 10 pupil sprawled on the floor. He had tripped and fallen hard against the door frame. Noha decided his arm was hanging 'limply' and he looked 'deathly pale'. Dr Awad did not even have to shout. One hard look 'terminated' the fight. He made the intruders line up against the wall, file into the room and sit at the back 'looking foolish'. "Could you run down to the Deputy's office," he asked Noha, "and tell him that Andy Grey has been seriously hurt?"

Apparently, "Mr Shaw was stuffing the foul remnant of an egg sandwich into his mouth". His eyes looked into Noha's, "dead cold and piercingly blue". Noha told him what had happened 'boldly'. She had to muster all her courage, but she looked straight back at him. Based on what Dr Awad had taught her, she decided his eyes were "cerulean". In a garbled memory of Blake, however, she sensed burning anger in them, "like a furnace of the night".

Before the Roll of Honour evening, Eydon Vale was always unstable: afterwards, there were days it felt safe. By the last week of the Easter Term, recorded Disciplinary Concerns was 330, half of where we started. Through noticing, praising and rewarding individuals' commitment and concentration, day in day out, moment by moment, we had been reshaping group behaviour.

What had also happened was that leadership had begun to emerge at all levels of the institution. Senior teachers like Kylie Lawrence, our Head of PE, assistants like Adam and pupils like Noha and Alice Lawton were putting in the extra effort and encouraging others to follow. Intellectual, creative and athletic progress was shadowing behavioural reforms. In the blog that Adam helped Noha write about her Easter School, he emphasised the growth of team spirit:

Noha was a middle-distance runner.
She would be trained in 400 metres,
half a mile and a mile.
But what she was looking forward to
was the fun run.

It was up the side of a mountain.
Wales was stunning.
At one point, the train tracks
ran next to the sea.
It passed old castles.
When she saw Snowdon,

her heart gave a leap.
There were mountains
where her grandfather trained
for his Olympic gold in her old country.

Noha did not feel lost or alone.
She had the odd feeling
she was coming home.
After the first meal,
Trevor Black gave a pep talk.
He had won gold for GB
and knew all about her granddad.

He told them all
to push themselves
harder than they had ever done
in their lives.
But he said they were a team.
They all had to look out
for each other.

Noha was always in the pack
at the front of each race.
After a couple of days,
it was clear to everyone
how fast Noha was.
No one her age came near her.
She was still only 14.
Yet she was faster
than any of the other under-15s.

But every day,
Noha had the feeling
it could all go wrong.
She was on a tight rope
and could fall off
at any moment.

That week in Wales
was like a dream come true for Noha.
The girls in her dorm
would steal out in the night.
They would go to the dining room
for midnight feasts.
They found a den in the grounds
and slept out in it.

They even found a frog
and put it in Trevor's bed.
Trevor laughed about it,
but he said there would be pay-back.
"Then the kids who had put it there
would be truly sorry."
Everyone chorused "Amen!" and laughed.

On the day of the fun run,
there was snow on the ground.
The hill fog had come down.
The under 15s set off
before the under 18s.
Noha led from the front.
Then the older ones
started catching her up.

As Harry passed her,
she stepped off the path.
She slipped on the ice
and fell hard.
She cried out in pain.

What was Noha to do?
If Noha stopped to help Harry,
she would lose the race.
But she could not leave her there
out in the cold.
Then an 18-year-old called Jane stopped.

She said, "Harry is my friend.
I'll look after her."
Noha decided to run back
to get help.
As she ran back down the track,
the other kids cheered
and cracked jokes.
None of them knew
what she was up to.

That night, Trevor spoke to them all.
Harry had not broken any bones.
But the hospital was
keeping her in
for checks.
It would be some time
before she could run again.

Trevor thanked Noha and Jane
for looking after her.
He let the others know
what they had done.
"They gave up all hope
of winning the race.
They knew the cost
of being team members!"
Everyone cheered.

Chapter Ten: Defusing Fights

We had a great start to the summer term. Rhiannon opened our Training Day by thanking all those who contributed to the Easter Holiday revisions classes. "Pupil attendance was excellent. The pupils worked hard, and the Mock Exam papers that I've seen have been very promising. "While all the classes were happening, we were also holding interviews for the new Head of Science. It's now my great pleasure to introduce Archie Laud. Some of you might remember Archie from the start of his career. He worked at Eydon Vale before taking up a post in the private sector overseas. His last job was in the Gulf, where he served as the Principal of an independent school."

Rhiannon went on, "I'm also pleased to tell you that, following representations from the Trustees, Dr Awad has been granted residency status by the Home Office. As most of you will know, he has been volunteering as a teaching assistant in Art. From now on he will become a fully paid member of the teaching staff. These two new appointments will go a long way towards reassuring Ofsted about the school's future."

After a round of applause and some ribald comments for Archie and Adam, Rhiannon introduced the day's speaker. Bea Wright was one of the first headteachers in the UK to adopt Guided Discipline. A stocky, slightly overweight woman with the lined face of a smoker, she had an uncompromising Northern Irish accent. Her face broke into a frank and unguarded smile, however, as she came into the school hall. Over the previous decade, she and I had worked together in several schools. Bea began by complimenting the staff on the progress they had already made.

Very few teachers and even fewer Inspectors would have had your experience of overcoming such chronic and extreme disruption. As you have shown, programmes like Guided Discipline can bring about a rapid fall in negative behaviour. What's so distinctive about our approach is that in leading by example, getting into the classroom and out onto the playground, senior managers can mould the package to suit their schools.

We are not just training pupils in unthinking obedience. We're creating a virtuous circle of constructive school norms, within which pupils can develop more appropriate work habits. As you will have noticed, they have begun to reflect more deeply; and engage in more serious discourse with one another. However, what I've been asked to do today is demonstrate some practical ways of intervening in fights.

I don't think it's an exaggeration to compare the spread of violence at turbulent schools to the transmission of a contagious virus. And I believe it can be suppressed through the adoption of public health strategies like those deployed in overcoming Ebola. What you have learned so far is how to damp down day-to-day instability. You have used rules, praise and sanctions to prevent and contain conflict before it turns violent. What we are about to focus on today are situations where young people have started to exchange blows.

I need to advise you never to intervene in playground altercations alone. Groups of two or preferably three teachers should walk directly and calmly towards the students as soon as they see them squaring up. They should also move in as quickly as they can whenever they see crowds gathering in the playground. The pupils on the edge of a fight have a role to play in stoking animosity. The bigger the group, the more serious the issue. The excitement of a brawl transmits itself so quickly. It spreads the contagion of violence and stokes the vicious cycle of destructive norms.

As in all animals, the threat of attack produces a hormonal cascade. You will all know about the fight/flight response. Adolescent skirmishes have a three-part pattern. The first stage is a confrontation; the second an exchange of blows; the third a lull. This cycle will be repeated until the less aggressive teen withdraws. If you can synchronise your approach with the first signs that one or another of the combatants may be about to take evasive action, you can turn these hormonal changes to your advantage.

You should repeat the instruction to back off. Once the students have started to grapple, you have to look to your own safety, though. Timing is crucial. The lull is the key. It allows staff to intervene most effectively. You need to approach the individuals at the first signs of a lull. The combatant who looks at the teacher first should be led away, as he or she is likely to be the less aggressive of the two.

The second adult should deal with the more belligerent pupil. Both students should be isolated, just as a doctor in a developing country would isolate the carriers of Ebola. It is the responsibility of the third, backup teacher to disperse the crowd. The bigger the audience, the harder it is for the combatants to lose face. The audience will want to wait until the show is over. So, the third member of staff has to keep repeating the direction energetically and calling crowd members by name to leave.

After her introduction, Ada showed us a video to demonstrate the three stages of a fight. Then she called for volunteers to act out the procedures in role play. John Sugar, the Kick Boxing PE teacher, took the lead role. A couple of his female colleagues conducted a slow-motion comedy fight, while Ada acted as the second duty teacher. She told the rest of the staff the fight was over, and they should immediately disperse. Rhiannon had Easter eggs ready to give out to the performers. There was a lot of good-natured banter during the morning break.

The second topic of the day was how to deal with class-wide toxic relationships and the 'bullying triangle' of victim, persecutor and rescuer. According to Ada, "victims see themselves as oppressed, helpless and hopeless. A person in the victim role will look for a rescuer. Rescuers work hard to help other people while neglecting their own needs. They are frequently overworked and can easily be pushed into martyrdom. Persecutors criticize and blame the victim, maintain their power through threats and bullying. What gives the bullying triangle so much of its power is that people will switch roles: victims turn on their rescuers and persecute them."

Then after lunch, Ada led a discussion on cell phones. "Even if the teacher is in control and the pupils keep their mobiles out of sight, the fact that it is in a pocket or bag makes it a distraction. They will be thinking about all the messages they are missing. As a staff, you need to agree on a common strategy for ensuring the phones are out of reach during lessons. First-time offenders need to know that the phones that you impound will be stored in a secure place until home time. And tougher sanctions will be needed for persistent offenders."

It was not long before the staff had an opportunity to test their new skills. Kylie Lawrence, the Head of PE, called me out of lunch to deal with "an interesting looking crowd" that had gathered in the playground. As Kylie told me, "It's not a fight, as such. Gerry Conlin is back. The previous Head threw him out in Year 9 for selling drugs. Since then, the kids say he's been working as an enforcer for the dealers."

Gerry had been to the front gate on a previous occasion, when the Head of History, had been on duty. Gerry had 'biked' him, driving his scooter directly at him. Kylie said she would deal with the crowd, exactly as Ada's DVD had suggested. The two of us walked slowly but directly towards Gerry. I kept repeating the instruction for Gerry to leave the playground. He ignored me until I was quite close. When I warned him that I would have to phone the police, Gerry turned his head and spat at me.

He then swore and started to ride off on his motorbike. Several teachers had by now emerged from the lunch hall. John Sugar and a couple of others joined Kylie in directing the crowd of pupils to disperse. As Gerry circled round, I held up my cell phone. Holding my mobile phone in my hand, I said in a loud voice, "I have already keyed in 999. If you do not leave the premises, I will contact the police. A squad car will be here within four minutes."

As Gerry rode at me, I spoke into my phone. Gerry turned off at the last moment and accelerated out of the playground. After Rhiannon appeared and emphasised that she had called the police, they scattered. A knot of Year 8s wanted to express their appreciation, though.

One of them told me, "You did not need to do that."

"You were awesome!" said another.

"He could have stabbed you!" a third.

As part of its responsibility for supporting Turbulent Schools, the Home Office had promised that the local constabulary would provide an immediate response to call-outs at Eydon Vale. In the event, it took three-quarters of an hour for a squad car to arrive. However, Rhiannon made a complaint about this delay and the next time the police were called out, they took just four minutes to appear.

This episode gave duty staff greater confidence with intruders. Having consulted the Chair of Trustees and Rhiannon, I was able to confirm that I would be prepared to go to court to testify against Gerry. The school's public stand against someone with as high a profile had a ripple effect through the community. Ex-pupils had been wandering onto the school grounds for years, intimidating staff and pupils, selling drugs, stealing and engaging in vandalism.

This problem now tailed off. Gerry Conlin pleaded guilty just before his case came to court and he was given a short Youth Custody sentence. The bill for glazing broken windows had been £17,000 the term before I arrived at Eydon Vale. That summer term, it fell below £2000.

Archie Laud started work that day as the new Head of Science. He had taught at Eydon Vale years before and knew how to talk to the children. I visited three of his lessons during the day to introduce him to the children and ensure he had all the rewards and lists of rules and sanctions he needed to apply Guided Discipline. He appeared to have great presence and his effect on the whole Science Tower was striking.

This had been the last remaining part of the building that we had failed to pacify. A succession of supply teachers had been using the topmost laboratory since the previous Head of Science went on long-term sick leave in November. Some had been more effective than others. But even when the strongest were in the lab, the pupils always made a noise, which echoed down the stairwell. Children were used to lounging on the landings and disrupting other Science lessons. The staircase itself was very narrow and after the initial riot, I had insisted that the Trust install a safety mesh to prevent the children from throwing each other over the bannisters.

As I climbed the stairs to see how Archie was coping, all was now quiet. He was not dictating notes or getting the pupils to copy from the board as James Thomas, the previous supply teacher, had done. He taught them confidently and they listened to him, thoroughly engaged in the lesson. Even on that first day, this also had the effect of calming the classrooms of the two supply teachers who shared the top landing. However, the next morning he telephoned Rhiannon to say he would not be returning.

For the Science staff and Senior Managers alike the news of his resignation was a terrible blow. Archie had been well-liked from his earlier stint at the school. Gina, the Acting Head of Science, was in tears. Luckily, there had been one other outstanding candidate at the interview who had been unable to start work until September. Our chances of passing the next Inspection hinged on our reaching a certain percentage of satisfactory lessons. With Archie Laud's help, we might have reached that figure.

When Sir Henry telephoned Archie later in the day to see if he could persuade him to change his mind, it was clear that he had only taken the job at Eydon Vale as a safety net. He had also been applying for Principals' posts ever since he left the Gulf. When he got home the previous night, there was a letter offering him the Headship of a prep school in Berkshire. They want him to start tomorrow. Sir Henry offered him an instant promotion to Assistant Head, but as he said, the removal vans are outside his house! Archie wanted Sir Henry to reassure Rhiannon that the children's behaviour had not put him off. He was sorry to have let us all down.

However, that was not how the staff or pupils felt. For many, this was a reminder of Eydon Vale's failure. The children whom he had taught on Monday had felt confident that he would help them make up lost ground with their exams. They worried that Eydon Vale pupils would never shake off their unteachable reputation. James Thomas, the supply teacher who had been taking Archie Laud's classes and who now returned to them had a very hard day. One of his groups simply refused to open their books for him.

"Two steps forward, one step back", as Rhiannon told the next morning's staff briefing philosophically.

Chapter Eleven: The Toxic Class

The uniformed policewomen who came to take my statement about Gerry Conlin apologised for the delay in sending out a squad car. Afterwards, they said they had heard how bad things had been at Eydon Vale. So, I persuaded them to take a tour of the classrooms, partly to reassure them how much calmer it now was and partly to show the pupils that we had police protection.

Partly as a result, more children began writing statements about playground issues. The day after the police came into school, a notorious bully was observed throwing coins. He denied doing it and confidently expected to bluff his way out of trouble. But our witnesses' statements allowed us to suspend him temporarily from school.

We also had more parental calls. The father of the first pupil to have been given a secret friend contacted me. Mr Appleby's older son Paul was complaining of verbal bullying by a group of girls in his form. I found it difficult to believe what he was saying at first. The girls he mentioned were among the most sensitive and talented in the year. Jane Williams had already reached Grade 6 in piano, while Isobel Macintyre played saxophone in a regional orchestra. They should have been a credit to any school.

When I tackled them about the complaint, they told me that there was a group of boys in the class, including Paul, who had been name-calling them in lessons and bullying them online. Dr Awad had just taken over as the group's form tutor, so I encouraged him to deal with the problem as if it were 'the toxic class syndrome'. This had been the subject of the second lecture that Bea Wright had given on the first day of the Summer Term.

Ada had argued that a few groups in all schools develop deep-rooted antipathies. As individuals, they had been hurt so often and so deeply they had opted for a game called 'getting your retaliation in first'. Quick to blame others, such pupils became defensive. They would never admit their shortcomings or accept conventional attempts at conflict resolution. In some schools, such problems could pass unnoticed for years.

In the following week's assemblies, I told the pupils about the bullying 'triangle', in which victims become persecutors and rescuers. I once again encouraged those who were stuck in destructive relationships to come forward.

"Just before the interview for this job last October, I came on a visit and stayed for lunch. It felt to me as if the attitude of the whole school was wrong. The place was noisy and rough. I sat down in the Hall and had a meal with a group of rude lads. They had no respect for me as a visitor, or for learning, or for what the staff were trying to do for them. When I asked what their advice would be to a new kid, they used expressions like: 'fight fire with fire' and 'don't let anyone even think they can hurt you'.

"How far we have come since then! Eydon Vale is so much more peaceful now. It has not completely recovered: we can all see that. At the moment, we could be compared to someone recovering from a serious fever. Most of the time, the temperature is close to normal, but every once in a while, it spikes again. And some classes are harbouring that nasty little virus. So, ask yourself: is your class toxic? If it is, come and tell me. And smile more. Show some positive attitude. Make Eydon Vale a friendlier place for visitors."

This allowed Dr Awad enough time to read up the articles that Bea Wright had recommended on 'no blame' procedures. The parents of the four girls' and the four boys they had accused were then telephoned and invited into school for a structured discussion about the online bullying that had blighted our tutor group. Most said that they did not know enough about their children's social media habits but offered their help in getting to the truth. Three of them, Mrs Williams, Mrs McIntyre and Mr Appleby, agreed to come in for a buffet lunch with the affected children in the Head's conference room.

All around the walls, Dr Awad had arranged a display of the pupils' artwork, together with some of his sketches of them in the Art Room. An attractive array of sandwiches and snacks had been laid on by the school's catering staff. As Edwina, the Head's Personal Assistant, helped me serve them, he explained that online problems were part of a pattern of name-calling and squabbling that had become endemic at Eydon Vale.

"All schools have a degree of bullying and name-calling, but this had been allowed to fester unchecked for far too long. A bad look or a word out of place is automatically met with a barbed reaction. Today's meeting is the school's way of accepting responsibility. It is predicated on the idea that none of your children is to blame for getting hooked into the cycle. If anyone is to blame, it's the adults for letting things get out of hand."

After the PA and I left, Dr Awad introduced the idea of 'No blame mediation'. What this involved was a series of statements. He would go round the circle, allowing each pupil to speak without interruption or blame. To start with, Dr Awad asked each pupil to say what it was that others in the room had done that he or she did not like. In the first round, Dr Awad asked that all the pupils be specific about names, times and words used. His only rule was that no one would be allowed to interrupt, respond or refute. They would all have to listen to the others' complaints in silence.

Jane Williams started. She mentioned the way Paul Appleby had sat behind her in Year 7, pulling her pigtails. When Dr Awad reminded her to describe exact dates, she had told the group about the way he had kept muttering "Slag" in a recent French lesson, plus the online messages he had sent her the week before. As each of the eight pupils described their own experiences, a picture emerged of historic physical bullying and present verbal abuse.

In the next round, Dr Awad gave all the pupils a chance to rebut any of the charges against them. There were minor criticisms of words used or timings, but overall, it was clear that all the pupils implicitly admitted giving others in the class a hard time. In the third round, Dr Awad asked each of them how they felt to be victims of this teasing and name-calling.

Discussing emotions was much harder for these Year 8s. Few wanted to admit how hurtful the verbal abuse had been. Jane took the first step. She said that she had known Paul since nursery school. Until she had arrived at Eydon Vale, she had thought he had liked her. In October of her Year 8, just before the old Head resigned, she had come home from school to find he had been sending her nasty photos and text messages. It had made her cry, though she did not tell anyone at the time, as she felt ashamed.

Her example encouraged the rest to be franker. Dr Awad then asked the three parents present to cross-question their own children about how they felt. Mrs Williams, Jane's mother, put her arm around her, then volunteered the fact that she had been bullied at school. She, too, had come home and wept in her bedroom. Her example encouraged Mrs

McIntyre, the other mother, to talk about her bad memories of school, and as the truth emerged about how painful it had been, both adults wept. As Dr Awad told me afterwards, it was striking to see how shocked the children were to see the adults' tears. This was a crucial moment. More than anything else, this sudden revelation of the parents' vulnerabilities helped them to understand what a mess things were. The adults' defences were down. The savagery at the heart of their children's class was clear for all to see.

As Dr Awad told me afterwards, he was cursing himself for not anticipating the need for paper handkerchiefs. "I had been highly apprehensive about mediating such a discussion. I was not sure if they would all trust me. I am a Syrian asylum seeker, new to teaching in an English state school. Yet, for the first time, I thought the children were beginning to understand how corrosive relationships have become. And the parents' honesty was so painful, it brought this home to us."

As the bell for the end of the lunchbreak sounded, and the pupils left the room with Dr Awad, I returned. I asked the two mothers and Mr Appleby how they felt about the future. He and Jane's mother were both positive and relieved, though Mrs McIntyre was dubious that the boys would change. They all expressed their thanks that there was no more physical bullying in the lessons and that it had almost stopped in the playground.

Mr Appleby told me, "You are only just beginning to consider the issues of verbal bullying. This is not a criticism: don't get me wrong. I think you are doing a superb job here, Mr Shaw. But you need to carry out a bullying audit across the whole school, to plumb the extent of the problem. You need to put all the pieces in the jigsaw together before you can see the whole picture. Dr Awad is exceptional, but you need to train up more teachers in how to do what he's done today."

"You've got to train many more," agreed Mrs Williams. "Dr Awad got the kids to lower their defences and listen to each other. He showed them respect. I just love his portrait of Jane. Do you think you could ask Dr Awad if he would let me take it home to show my husband?"

Much of the anger that had characterised the original parents' forum in December had dissipated by the time Rhiannon called another Forum for the Summer Term. It was the fourth such meeting since Eydon Vale went into Special Measures. The first comment came from Jane

Williams's mother. She wanted to know why there were never any school plays or musicals anymore. Other parents were also upset about the loss of key staff, and several raised the recent collapse of German lessons. Even so, most appreciated the hard work that the children and teachers had put in since Christmas.

As Rhiannon contrasted the end of the Christmas Term and its massive flour fights with the calm of the previous week, one parent asked, "How far does Ofsted expect a school like Eydon Vale to come in just one term?"

In answer, Rhiannon asked me to describe the public speaking exercise that she had witnessed that morning. The Acting Head of English and I had brought our Year 10s together. The two top sets had had a debate on Brexit. Neither had had much practice in formal speaking and listening, but the progress they had made was remarkable.

"All my experience suggests that adolescents develop the skills of argument quite naturally," I told the parents. "Eydon Vale pupils are particularly good at anticipating what the other side will say and getting their retaliation in first. You may have noticed this at home."

There was a ripple of indulgent laughter in the hall, and even Mrs Williams smiled.

"We had built our preparation around this. We had taught the pupils to create a line of argument around the weaknesses in what they thought the opposition would say. What issues might the other side be trying to hide? What flaws should they expect in their arguments? How could humour be employed to make them look silly? How could a more sophisticated vocabulary make their arguments sound stronger?

"There were three main speakers on each side, and then the debate was thrown open to the floor. Even the pupils in the audience had written a speech in full for homework and learned it. The majority had started with the belief that we should have an immediate clampdown on immigration, even if it meant a hard break with Europe. However, the more research they carried out on the economic costs and the more closely they listened to the other side, the more they understood how complex the issues were.

"When the pupils voted, 31 supported hard Brexit, and 29 opposed it. It was thrilling for me to watch them come to grips with the other side's point of view. They were learning how to use statistics, logic, feeling and rhetorical devices to gain the upper hand - rather than brute force. They were so pleased with themselves that, in the end, they even voted to revive the Eydon Vale Debating Society, with Tom Windsor as President."

There was tittering in the audience as I mentioned Tom's name. Even Rhiannon smiled at my naïveté.

"Before you came, Mr Shaw, Tom Windsor was one of the worst bullies here," explained one of the parents.

"Well, it looks as if he's quite a reformed character now. I'd guess that an Ofsted Inspector listening to him speak in the debate would have been just as excited as I was. The lesson would have been graded as 'good' at the very least."

"Why not 'excellent'?" called out another parent.

"Good question! I'm no Inspector, so I can't be sure. Compared to the Year 11 top sets, who have had the benefit of all the extra lessons and holiday classes, the Year 10s are still finding it difficult to plan their essays. They keep on looking around the room in order to think of what they want to write. They need the skill of thinking and writing at the same time. However, there was no mistaking the fact that they were more composed, enthusiastic and alert than the Year 11s were six months ago. To put my answer another way: Ofsted doesn't give marks for trying."

The parents burst into laughter, which turned into applause.

The promised "mini inspection" took place in early May. Christian Dean and Neil Burton, an Ofsted Inspector from a neighbouring borough, came in for a day's observations. Christian mainly concentrated on behaviour management. He thought that the progress we had made so far was "heartening". There had been a "real improvement", particularly in movement around school and pupil behaviour in the playground. There was evidence of a "reasonably consistent approach to the Guided Discipline policy, even amongst supply staff".

Not only were the behaviour and attitude of the children much improved, but there were also signs of growing maturity. However, there were still isolated examples of extreme indiscipline and violence. Most stemmed from the learned behaviour of a tiny subgroup of pupils across the age range. These pupils were only just being contained at this point.

Christian was critical of the completion of competency procedures for permanent teachers with deep-rooted problems. Rhiannon had invested a huge amount of time trying to fast track the termination of the contracts of the staff on long term sick leave, but the latest, much-vaunted government procedures did not appear to work.

Christian was also scathing about the lack of support from other schools in the Trust. There was little to show for the efforts of Rhiannon and Sir Henry. Each academy had been invited to seconding at least one teacher, with excellent discipline and a proven track record in getting results, but only one had delivered. The single special school had offered us materials for a basic literacy training programme, but no staff to go with them.

He reserved his most devastating criticism for our special needs provision. The SENCo's absence rate was particularly high. She was failing to set a good example to other staff in her relations with the difficult children in her Year 7 class. Her procedures and paperwork were disorganised. Christian had seen the film that the IT technician had made about Laura Aspen's class and singled it out for praise. Why not use it in a training programme for the whole staff?

He suggested we make a similar film of Angela Clayton's lessons. A Parent Governor, she had taken over as Acting Head of English in December, following the long-term absence of the Head of Department. Angela's review of the mock exam that the targeted pupils had done in the Easter holidays indicated a range of problems and she asked me if I could do anything with Clara Salt.

Clara had been absent for most of the Christmas Term's work on Shakespeare. She was a brilliant though particularly demanding pupil. I phoned Clara at home and we agreed that the only way she would pass Literature GCSE would be to spend all day, every day concentrating on Romeo and Juliet. She would watch a video of the key scene, analyse a key section of the text and draft an exam essay in the morning. She would repeat the exercise in the afternoon.

We cleared one of my office tables and with each day that passed her concentration and commitment grew. If I happened to be in my office, she would pass me her work and ask for my comments. Normally a prickly student, she accepted my criticisms more readily than I had expected. She even stayed at school late into the evenings. The only other lessons she attended that week were ICT, Maths and my top set English group's.

By Friday afternoon, Clara appeared close to exhaustion. Her eyelids began to quiver and I thought she might fall asleep. However, by home time, she was full of life again and chattering to Angela Clayton about how her boyfriend was taking her out to dinner. She and one other pupil were going to sleep over at Angela's house on Saturday and Sunday, to ensure they revised their Literature for the following week's exam.

I was asked to deputise for the head at the final Governors' meeting of the term. Rhiannon's son had been rushed to hospital that afternoon. For reasons I failed to appreciate at the time, she was reluctant for me to stand in for her, so she had asked Brian Smithson. He happily accepted this was my responsibility, though.

The main agenda items covered discipline, exclusions and finance. As Chair, Jacob Hornsby encouraged a lengthy discussion on the apparent improvement in the attitudes and behaviour of the pupils. Colin Pilgrim, a local vicar and the Vice-Chair of the Governors, reported that his parishioners agreed the school was now a safe, quiet place, where the pupils could concentrate on their work. The GCSE exams were about to start and he, for one, was looking forward to Results Day.

Chapter Twelve: Transforming Special Provision

The Ofsted team that put Eydon Vale into Special Measures had criticised the high rates of semi-literacy and the large numbers who left with no GCSEs. But apart from that, they had shown little interest in Special Needs provision. They had not even visited its Special Unit and there were no complaints about cutbacks to therapy. Now that our extra lessons for more able Year 11s were coming to an end, I took my plans for a radical transformation of Special Provision to Enaya Blake. She was the teacher in charge of the Special Unit and one of the few gifted teachers at Eydon Vale.

Enaya had been at Eydon Vale for five years. Her original intention had been to encourage inclusion. There would be a free flow of pupils into and out of the unit. She had wanted her students to receive some of their lessons in the mainstream, and in return, she would teach mainstream pupils with poor literacy. However, as school discipline deteriorated, she lowered her sights. The previous Head had always envisaged her unit as a mini special school and was happy for her to concentrate on her "statemented pupils".

When I joined Eydon Vale, there were five Special Needs posts. Its Special Needs Coordinator seemed to have been overwhelmed by the new education, health and care plans (EHCPs). She divided her time between paperwork and a small group of Year 7 pupils with low SATs scores. She had regular, lengthy absences and was on Rhiannon's list for competency procedures.

For the older pupils, there were six unqualified special needs assistants. Their main job was not to support the inclusion of children with EHCPs, but baby-mind recalcitrant mainstream pupils. They would sit silently in judgement over the discipline of the staff and pass on their complaints to their manager. Their manager used to report these to the previous Head every morning. As behaviour improved, there was less need for these SEN assistants and Rhiannon had terminated most of their contracts.

When I shared my ideas for transforming SEN provision with Rhiannon, she was unenthusiastic. "You need to be careful. The parents will assume your changes will come at the expense of the more able. Reform rarely comes from the bottom of the ability range. If you boost the kids at the top, the improvements in their exam grades will drag all the others up with them. We live in an unequal society. That's how it works."

"True. That's why we started with all the extra classes for the ablest students. And what I had in mind is relatively small scale. I would just be asking Enaya to team teach with half a dozen volunteers from the mainstream and use their experience as a springboard for integration. If it works, we can get more staff working with the mainstream pupils who would otherwise leave school with no GCSEs."

Rhiannon reluctantly agreed to an after-school training session the following week. I started by showing the staff a series of slides about long term deindustrialisation on Holmesside and the loss of unskilled and semi-skilled jobs. "The only hope for our school leavers lies in a radical shift in teachers' skills and attitudes. The more able at Eydon Vale can see a way out through extra classes and improved GCSE exam results. They understand where their interests lie. The better their results become, the more their behaviour improves. But for the least able, there needed to be a completely new approach.

"What I would like is to train up a small group of volunteers. Now the Year 11s are on study leave, we'll start one-to-one SEN support in those slots. First, they would work with mainstream pupils on basic literacy. The second step would be for the volunteers to team-teach their subjects in the Special Unit. We have a vibrant special class here at Eydon Vale, but its pupils never join mainstream classes. What I would like is to allow mainstream staff to teach a few lessons to the Unit children in their subject specialisms, as a precursor to the part-time inclusion of these pupils. Enaya Blake has agreed to allocate each of them one or two pupils.

"Every year, we'd train a new set of volunteers. Hopefully, they will come from across the curriculum. The spreading of expertise and involvement among a wider group of adults means that the pupils continue to make long-term progress, even after the help had been withdrawn. Only when there is a critical mass of secondary subject staff who have had this experience can we begin to call the school inclusive."

Spelling out these ideas had a disturbing effect on the staff. While they had readily accepted the need for Guided Discipline and extra exam lessons for the more able, they found inclusion more challenging. Until now there had been an unspoken assumption, fostered by the previous

Head, that the Government had removed "the bias towards integration". They resented the loss of their SEN assistants and did not want to resume responsibility for their more troublesome pupils. And they did not want to give up their free periods to teach children to read. As my training session ended, they left in stunned silence.

It was clear from the feedback I received over the next few days that while they enjoyed the slides and understood the PowerPoints, a significant minority baulked at my message. It was as if the training session's central theme - that all staff needed to become teachers of special needs - came as a complete surprise. By the end of the week, the entire History and Geography departments had resigned.

In the discussions that followed the training session, the only teacher in the Humanities Faculty to come to the support of this new strategy had been Rowena Cross. She was the RE specialist who had been tempted to leave teaching after a pupil had spat in her coffee mug the previous term. Rowena was disgusted with her colleagues' attitude. Like Rhiannon, they were more concerned about the way that our reforms, which until now had favoured the pupils likely to get the best GCSE scores, would affect the school's image.

After meeting with Enaya Blake, Rowena asked if she could join this group of Special Needs volunteers. She already had a job lined up in another school, but she saw this reshaping of special provision as a way of broadening her teaching skills. Over the final eight weeks of the year, she would learn the basics of initial literacy, team-teach Religious Education in the Special Unit and integrate two of its pupils in her regular Year 8 lessons.

The two she was allotted were Elroy Samson's brother Kev and a girl with cerebral palsy called Sylvie Francome. Both were outspoken and keen to integrate. For their first mainstream lesson, Rowena had opted for an adventurous, open-ended discussion about the afterlife. At the start, a sizeable group said they believed in reincarnation. There was also a significant minority who hoped that they would be able to meet loved ones in heaven. Sylvie needed little encouragement to tell the class about the kind of spiritual experience Rowena recognised from her Master's dissertation.

"My mother and I were in a car accident before I was born. She was so badly injured, that her body was only kept alive by the ambulance crew.

She was brain dead, and the oxygen flow to my brain was affected. That's why I am as disabled as I am. She died before I was born, but I feel she is still with me. She is my guide and protector, even though she is dead." The other pupils looked at Sylvie with new respect. Her transparency disarmed them. Her anecdote prompted the only Nigerian in the school, a boy called Aki, to put his hand up. He told the class about the night his baby brother died.

"I was on a night train from the north of the country to Lagos with my father. In the middle of the night, we were both woken up. I asked my dad the time. It was 2:22. He told me to go back to sleep, but I lay awake for hours tossing and turning. I knew something was wrong. When our train stopped in Lagos the next morning, my mother was there to meet us. She told us that my little brother had died at 2:22."

Once again, all the pupils fell silent. No one else knew what to say, so Kev put his hand up. He decided he was going to tell the class about the night he had seen his father's ghost in the tunnel of trees at the edge of town.

Afterwards Miss Cross asked, "Do you believe in ghosts, Elroy?"

"I never used to, Miss. I used to think that when we die, that's it, but now I feel my dad is still with me, just like Sylvie said."

Another of the teachers to join this voluntary group was Elinor Tully, the Head of Music. Elinor was a single parent in her mid-thirties, with a careworn face, kindly eyes and long grey hair, tied back in a bun. When she had first come to Eydon Vale, she had organised the music for school plays. In the previous couple of years, the drama teacher had moved on, Elinor's husband her left her, and the pupils' keyboards had been stolen. It was a miserable time. As the school had descended into chaos, she lost heart.

Elinor had to accept that her initial training had never prepared her for coping for work in such a turbulent school. After the first lecture on Guided Discipline, she redesigned her curriculum. With far fewer instruments for the pupils to play, she abandoned her old programme of study and spent more time on choral singing. This new approach made it easier for her to set boundaries and use rewards. As good order returned, so did her spirit of adventure. When I asked for volunteers for this new-style special needs provision, she had offered her services.

She had never taught children with moderate learning difficulties or physical impairments before, but with Enaya Blake's assistance, her efforts to teach music to the children in the special unit were an immediate success. It was more of a challenge to help the two semi-literate traveller children that she was allotted to read and write. So, I gave her a teaching project on the Magic Carpet theme. This included a chapter on phonics, linked exercises on planning and redrafting, writing frames and the direct teaching of sentence punctuation.

As she told me, "I'd never taught the 3Rs before. When I went to college, none of the lecturers thought secondary school musicians would ever need to know about that. But these days, we are all teachers of children with special needs. Mrs Blake has given me so much help in teaching phonics. And I'd like to rewrite your programme of study so that it combines listening to music, reading and the creation of a multi-media novel on the Magic Carpet theme."

Elinor began teaching her SEN pupils letter/sound correspondences and their 100 key words as soon as study leave for her GCSE Music class started. She had worked out how to split the Magic Carpet story into six separate chapters, which could be worked on week by week over the next half term. "Week One is finding the carpet," she told me. "Miss Starr has also promised that I could pull some of the gifted and talented mainstream pupils out of their other lessons for one-to-one singing lessons, too. I am not promising anything, but they are keen to put on an Abba concert this coming Christmas."

Over the weeks that followed, the basic skills of the two traveller children under Elinor's care would be transformed. Jonas and Michaela were amongst the most confused and demoralised pupils in Eydon Vale. They rarely arrived at their lessons on time, and neither carried a pen. They had never bothered with timetables. They used to visit the school office to find out where they should go to every lesson. As Jonas told Elinor, "Why d'you learn teachers' names if all you get are supply and they only last a week?"

On the first of these lessons, Elinor announced that they would be writing a long story in six parts over the next half term. She expected them to write at least 1000 words. The primary target for each lesson was 100 words. There were gasps of disbelief, "But I can't write, Miss!" She carried on regardless. She would reward the first who wrote ten lines. If they met the baseline target of 100 words, they would be given a merit slip to take home.

Elinor reminded the pupils of the school rules about listening to staff and not calling out. She then bombarded them with a rapid-fire, problem-solving exercise about finding the carpet: "When did you find the carpet? Where? Who was with you?" and so on. She then encouraged more extended contributions, allowing each of the small group to make a full oral rehearsal of the chapter, with descriptive details. As they started writing, Elinor played them inspirational extracts from Arabic classical music, Scheherazade and Steppenwolf.

Jonas Smith, a Roma with a poor history of attendance and behaviour, wrote 558 words in his first lesson. Michaela, who came from a settled family, managed just over 200. Elinor was delighted with the rapid progress they had made and the original details in their writing. They were enthusiastic about the redrafting lessons, too, illustrating the booklets they had produced on the computer and adding music and sound effects.

Chapter Thirteen: The Prom

Because of other commitments at the Town Hall, Rhiannon missed the Special Needs Training. She was seriously alarmed at the response. With few exceptions, she had been arriving at Eydon Vale after morning briefing all through the Easter Term. Her priority had been to drive her own two children to a private school several miles from Holmesside.

After the SEN evening, there was a change in her routine. Rhiannon took to arriving at Eydon Vale before me. Whenever I saw her car parked up in the space outside my office, I knew she would want to rebuke me. There was always someone on the staff whom I had irritated. She would tell me that my feedback on one teacher's discipline was unfair, or that I had rudely interrupted a staffroom conversation.

In exasperation one morning she said, "You have absolutely no management skills, Mr Shaw. You tell us not to be abrasive with the kids. But you just want to tell it like it is. No varnishing. No tact. Managing staff is a business. It has its own language. We don't get to make the rules."

I must have smiled when I said, "I thought that's exactly what we are doing here, Rhiannon," because she bristled. She continued to reprimand me but never spoke as openly again.

When I confided all this to Jacob Hornsby, the Chair of Governors, on the evening of the fourth Parents' Forum, he brushed my concerns aside. He told me not to let Rhiannon upset me. The parents had every confidence in what I was doing. He was chairing the Forum. His tone was positive. He told the parents that the Trust had ruled out closure. Work on the New Eydon had started and the building should be open by the new academic year.

There were three reasons for this. Firstly, the Leadership Team had already brought about "huge improvements" and the school had taken "a giant step forward". Secondly, the town was "bursting at the seams with children" and "there was nowhere else for them to go". And thirdly, the local town council had, at last, declared their opposition to the closure of Eydon Vale.

The new school would be based on strong discipline and a relentless pursuit of excellence in the classroom. At Ofsted's initial visit the previous November, they had declared that the "normal ethos of a school, where pupils come to school to learn" had broken down. Since

January, the Senior Management Team had been projecting a style of leadership that was more value-driven and underpinned with a stronger ethos. He specifically mentioned the Christian Aid assembly and the local Quakers' training programme in conflict resolution.

Jacob's Deputy Chair of Governors, Colin Pilgrim, was a local vicar. Colin was a generous, public-spirited man, with experience as a primary school teacher, child therapist and Governor in several schools. He had offered to lead a Year 7 Assembly for Christian Aid Week. The children filed in off the playground and sat silently in the Hall in perfect order. After an introduction from Rhiannon, Colin spoke about the importance of singing together and working together.

Elinor Tully, the school's Music teacher, then took the Year 7 through the Gospel Song she had been teaching some of the classes in their music lessons. There were two-part harmonies and lively dynamics. Some of the classes had learned the actions and Sign Language to go with the words. They swayed from side to side with the beat, and quite a few of them put heart and soul into it. For a moment, the assembly took off, lifting the children out of their everyday selves. Colin finished with a short prayer on behalf of Christian Aid.

To the casual observer, this assembly might not have appeared particularly out of the ordinary, but for us, it was a breakthrough. Colin said he had found the experience nerve-wracking and as he came out, his first words were, "Well, I'm still alive!" He did say that he would be happy to lead another assembly, though. The feedback from the Year 7 pupils was positive. One or two said they found the singing "embarrassing", but the great majority had enjoyed it. For their Form Tutors as well, it made "a nice start to the day".

In the previous week's discussions with the School Council about bullying, the pupils had asked that the school try to get the support of outside agencies to teach pupils how to defuse conflicts and resolve playground bullying. The success of our assembly with an Anglican vicar encouraged a local Quaker group to contact us. As part of their Peace Testimony, they were offering children and young adults training in Conflict Resolution.

The workshops would concentrate on developing the listening and negotiating skills of the pupils, helping them to understand anger, the way they respond to strong feelings, the choices they had and the strategies they could use in difficult situations. Holmesside Quakers offered us a package of sessions as an immediate response to the audit on bullying that we had just carried out.

The relative calm Eydon Vale was experiencing as the GCSE exams began was allowing a new kind of intellectual and spiritual life to emerge, especially where teachers with real flair were beginning to take risks. A new vitality was burgeoning in the school. But there was also an awareness of the awesome forces we all still had to deal with, both in the school and within ourselves.

I visited all the classrooms during the first period's PHSE, or Personal, Social and Health Education lesson that week. After my warnings to the staff about the importance that Ofsted would attach to these lessons, over 90% were settled and productive. The children were facing their teachers, with their outdoor jackets off. They were either listening to their instructions or engaged in discussions. There was an atmosphere of safety and well-being.

I had asked all the Heads of Year to ensure the form tutors received the pack of work on bullying I had prepared well before the lesson started, so they had enough time to read through them before the lesson. Elinor Tully's was fairly typical. The children in her class, like Talbot, singled out as bullies in our audit, found the exercise disturbing. But there was a sizeable minority who thought some kind of violence was inevitable: we were making too much fuss about bullying. One of the girls suggested that if I caught anyone making sexist remarks, he should be put in a circle of girls and asked to account for himself. This led to a lively early morning debate.

Some pupils in Dr Awad's class argued that we were failing to distinguish between good-natured fun, fair fights, "mucking about" and bullying. Others were unconvinced by the evidence of racism in our audits. They thought the very idea of white privilege outrageous, an example of exaggerated political correctness. This was countered by pupils who said that anyone who disagreed with the findings was in denial.

Because Eydon Vale had been designated a "turbulent" school, the Secretary of State required weekly reports from the moment it failed its inspection. Christian Dean had been hired to compile these reports. His role was to pass on Ofsted-style observations to the Department, the Trust and the Local Education Authority. An amiable and farsighted educationalist, he liked nothing better than to chat informally. The language he used with me was quirky and illuminating and quite at odds with "Ofsted speak". Having heard my ideas about vertigo, he used the concept of "wobbling" to describe the subjective experience of the staff in one of the briefing papers from this time:

Factors such as Friday afternoons, lessons after PE and bad weather days often show weaknesses in lesson plans that generally work. All teachers sometimes have unsatisfactory lessons. I have seen a teacher use the same plan with one class and have a satisfactory lesson, but the same lesson, given by the same teacher produced an unsatisfactory outcome with another. A well taught didactic lesson may well succeed with a well-motivated group, but not with a poorly motivated one. Even the best teachers will "wobble". On a larger scale, the whole school may undergo a "wobbly day". If mishandled at a school like Eydon Vale, this could generate a riot. However, it need not be a disaster, so long as the senior staff pick up the "wobbles" quickly and dampen them down.

Rhiannon thought that his reports put off the hour of the formal HMI re-inspection. When the Year 11s went on study leave and the great majority of the supply teachers' contracts were terminated, Christian estimated was that at least 85% of lessons were satisfactory or better. There was no doubt that our regular teachers were taking an increasingly consistent approach to Guided Discipline.

Several staff were taking their new-found confidence to job interviews and gaining promotion elsewhere. The previous Head had paid incentive allowances to retain good staff. Having played their part in helping Eydon Vale through the worst, they now felt as if they deserved more recognition. They did not relish the prospect of further years of hard work. They wanted to advance their careers with better paid jobs in less demanding schools. Eydon Vale had huge debts, so we could not have paid any more "retention" points, even if we wanted to.

Christian dropped a hint that successful internal exam scores might help us win over the HMIs. Exams had always presented problems for Eydon Vale School. There was anecdotal evidence from previous years that GCSE pupils had barracked invigilators and openly refused to work. The previous year, most had finished well before the allotted time. This year, the children's attitude and behaviour appeared to be the best ever. So when the main external exams were over, we decided to hold internal exams in the halls and gym.

Most children lined up quietly. They were allowed inside one at a time and marked off the register. They took off their coats and went to their designated desks, where starter materials were waiting for them. The great majority of the children wrote swiftly and with concentration until 10 minutes before the end, and about a quarter were still working when told to put their pens down. They left the hall quietly row by row. This was the first example of any large-scale event I had seen at Eydon Vale that had run smoothly.

Not everything went to plan, though. Lee Doonan, a pupil with a history of behavioural difficulties and long-term absences had no intention of doing the exams. He was riding his bike down the corridors when I picked him up. He refused to stop and gave his name as "Cuckoo". When I introduced myself and told him I was the school's new Deputy, he swore at me and rode off. He then poked his head around the exam hall doors, shouting inside and deliberately disrupting the exam. Brian Smithson notified the LEA of this problem and he was excluded for the maximum number of days allowed in the year.

The Parents' Forum that followed the exams was electrifying. One grandmother interrupted Sir Henry to tell the audience that no one in the leadership team, except for Mr Shaw, knew how to sort the school out. Her granddaughter had come home that lunchtime complaining of bullying. She did not want to come back to Eydon Vale ever again. Everyone now knew who the bullies were. Why was Miss Starr not excluding them?

Rhiannon said she was negotiating with the LEA for the removal of more pupils, but this was a slow process, and took up a lot of the school's budget. This did not go down well. The parents were in no mood for excuses. One specifically named a troublemaker with a history of drug-taking, bullying, violence and truancy. What was Mr Shaw going to do about him and his friends?

In answer, I explained the most recent changes in the children's behaviour during break and lunchtimes. Undesirable, ex-pupils had been indeed been making a habit of coming onto the school playground, to sell drugs and threaten non-payers. Three had come on-site one lunchtime the previous week. After we had called the police, they had jumped over the two-metre, metal stake fence at the back and thrown bottles into the playground. A squad car had arrived within 4 minutes and the police had taken the details. The boys had been cautioned and there had been no further incursions.

Given the grandmother's remarks at the start of the meeting, I sensed that Rhiannon would have been irritated by anything I said. My stories of derring-do at the school gates may have been insufferable, but they did have the effect of calming the meeting. The parents did not want to know what was supposed to be happening. They did not want pie in the sky. They wanted a narrative that reflected how things were in the classrooms and playground.

So, even though I sensed Rhiannon might think I was grandstanding, I described the way break time interactions had changed. Back in January, the playground had been full of sudden, freakish movements. Children used to run from group to group, pushing and hitting each other. As soon as a fight had broken out, knots of children had gathered to watch. This milling around had now virtually stopped, and the children played and chatted in stable groups most days.

I also told the meeting about the School Council's latest initiative. It had suggested that we get the support of agencies outside of school to give the children practical help in recognising and defusing verbal conflict. The "secret friends" initiative had done wonders for non-verbal bullying. Our present plan was for these agencies to train the next generation of pupil helpers, whom we would nickname our "Guardian Angels". We wanted a high-tech approach, with a Guardian Angels' website, which the victims could contact anonymously. When Rhiannon called the meeting to a close, everyone burst out clapping.

Ofsted or no Ofsted, the Year 11 GCSE exams had been going even better than we had hoped. The second English Literature paper, where the candidates had to compare unseen poems, passed off particularly well. Levels of concentration were high and 90% of the pupils continued to write until the last 5 minutes. Two of the cleverest pupils burst into tears as they left the exam hall, convinced they had misread a question. They were quite wrong, but they had been so tense that chance remarks by other pupils had crushed them.

It was not until mid-June that Rhiannon heard when our next Inspection would be. Two HMIs would be visiting the school for two days. Their remit would be to determine how much progress the school had made since it went into special measures and to determine its long-term viability. It was unknown for failing comprehensive schools to come out of special measures within the first inspection cycle. The database that we had constructed to record the kind of incidents "causing serious concern" had shown a steady decline. In our worst week, we had had 666 complaints. This had dropped to 330 by early June and it fell to 191 in the week before the inspection.

Rhiannon asked me to assemble a group of pupils for the Iona Salomon interview. The Year 11s had had their final Maths exam in the morning. In answer to the HMI's question about how well the paper had gone, Gillian Newsome grimaced. "The syllabus changed when we were halfway through Year 10, Miss. There were several questions none of us could answer. We all went to the extra lessons after school with the new Head of Maths. All his staff put on lunchtime groups to help us with particular topics, too. Some like Elroy here have also been having personal tutoring. But..."

"And in what other ways has the school changed since Christmas, Elroy?"

"In the old days, Eydon Vale was racist and sexist. No girl or black kid ever felt safe. Without real leadership from the previous Head, the staff were lost. The first day I was here, someone slashed me in a Maths lesson. There was no real investigation. Now we have the secret friends strategy, no one's afraid to tell Mr Shaw who the bullies are, and that's what has made Eydon Vale a safe school: simple as that. There's still a bit of name-calling, but the physical violence has gone and there's much less bullying here than in my supposedly 'outstanding school' in London."

"So there has been a big change in the ethos of the school?" suggested the HMI.

One of the Year 10s explained the difference between secret friends and all the anti-bullying strategies the previous head had tried. "So, Mr Shaw is pretty strict with the sanctions?" asked Mrs Salomon.

"We had decided to put a stop to racism ourselves. Mr Shaw did not want any of the kids taking the law into their own hands and I got caught in the February holiday school. I thought I was going to be permanently excluded. My whole future hung in the balance because, for Mr Shaw, good relationships come before League Tables."

"The last time that Eydon Vale was inspected, none of the pupils seen by the inspectors thought they were going to get decent exam results," said the Inspector. "From what you are saying, that is still true?"

"No, miss, Elroy did not mean that. You are putting words in his mouth," Gillian interrupted. "We've had extra lessons every night of the week, Saturday mornings and during the holidays since Christmas. Mr Shaw does his fair share and he's got the other teachers fired up, too. Just because you go to a failing school, you don't have to be a failure."

"It must have been quite a roller-coaster ride for you?" suggested Mrs Salomon. "How do you younger pupils feel? Is the education you are given here as good as what's on offer in other schools?"

Jonas, one of the traveller children, for whom Elinor Tully had been providing extra literacy lessons, caught her eye. "How do you like Eydon Vale?"

"Not much. I hate all the schools I go to. I skive as often as I can, but my reading has come on here: no question. I used to hate writing, too, but Mrs Tully wanted me to show you the book I am writing." And he passed Mrs Salomon the novel about the Magic Carpet.

"Do any others have extra reading and writing help?" Mrs Salomon asked.

"I do, Miss," Noha said.

"You must be the runner I've heard so much about? How has Eydon Vale helped you?"

"Until I came to this school, no one had ever given me any real help with my running. Mrs Lawrence offered to be my personal trainer. She worked with me three nights a week after school. She and Mr Shaw fixed it for me to go to a training camp for Future Olympians in Wales over the Easter holidays. The fees were all paid by the Lottery Fund. Thanks to their support, I am now the fastest miler in the UK for my age."

"Really? That's cool! And did you ever have to put up with any bullying?" asked the Inspector.

"No, Miss, I've never had a problem. No one would have dared say anything, thanks to Elroy and his crew. He protected all the black kids. One lunchtime, I watched one of the boys in my year throw a water bag at an African kid in the playground. It had pee-pee in it. When he went back into the boys' loo to refill it, I heard screams. I saw Elroy and his crew come out, followed by Simon with blood on his face. I put two and two together and made five. I thought I owed it to Mr Shaw to tell him what I thought I'd seen. He'd been so kind to me about the training camp. So, I grassed Elroy up."

Everyone in the conference room held their breath. How would Elroy react? His sudden burst of laughter broke the tension and the pupils relaxed. "It's true that we were waiting in the loo for Simon, but we did not lay a finger on him," he explained. "When he saw us in there, he panicked, tried to run away, slipped over and banged his own nose!" This led to relieved laughter. As the bell rang for the end of the lunch break, Elroy held up his hand and asked Mrs Salomon outright, "Are you going to close our school?"

She looked away and snapped her handbag shut. "It's not up to me," the HMI said. "But what I can tell you is that the school seems a lot safer than it used to be. It's not perfect. I have seen one or two awful lessons, but the great majority of pupils are working harder. You have convinced me how the use of secret friends like Noha has reduced bullying. I suspect that this has had a crucial effect on retention rates, as hardly any students are leaving Eydon Vale for other schools in the town, anymore. Under Ofsted guidelines, we are not allowed to tell you this is a good school, but the change is dramatic, I have to admit."

In the euphoria that followed the inspectors' visit, Rhiannon announced that we were going to have a Leavers' Prom. She ensured it was well planned and executed. The out of town hotel where it was held provided a disco, buffet and bouncers, who would stop the children wandering off to the other pub in the village, check the toilets and help the Eydon Vale staff manage behaviour. All the adults in the school were invited. They and over 100 Year 11 pupils paid £15 for a ticket.

Many schools in special measures serve areas of high deprivation, and an occasion like this would have been impossible for them without additional sponsorship from local firms. However, most of our families were only too happy to pay for all the extras. Several young people hired tuxedos or bought long dresses. They felt they deserved a good night out, so they had visited the hairdressers and hired stretch limousines. One young man, who had removed his shirt in what may have been the first stage of a striptease, was immediately surrounded and told to get dressed by the other pupils. But that was the limit of their misbehaviour.

The pupils knew what to expect and behaved accordingly. What made the evening such a success was the way adults and pupils got on together so well. There were 50 teachers, long-term agency staff, in-class support assistants and secretaries present and they danced and chatted with the pupils amiably.

My wife accompanied me to the prom. As I tried to make an introduction, though, Rhiannon walked straight past her. Perhaps she had other things on her mind, I thought to myself. Yet I couldn't help being reminded of Hanif Megat's warning about the cockpit.

Chapter Fourteen: New Executive Head

After the inspectors told us how dramatic the improvement in behaviour had been, the rhythm of school life slowed. Eydon Vale began to have good days, rather than good quarters of an hour. There were two high points over the summer holiday. The first was at the Amateur Athletics Youth Games, where Noha was slated for the girls' 1500 metres. She came first in her heats for the under 15s. And then she was on the top step of the podium at the medals' ceremony, wrapped in the Union Jack.

Results Day was the second peak. In the past, depressingly few children had turned up. This year, the foyer filled quickly and there was a long, anxious queue stretching outside, well before the students were meant to arrive. The results were even better than our target and by far the best in the school's history. As the pupils filed through the secretariat, picking up their exam returns from Rhiannon, there were hugs, tears and squeals of excitement.

When Elroy opened his results, he raised his fist in the air and shouted, "Yes!" He had done better than he had dared hope. He had got Grade 8s in English and Literature, 6 in Maths and top grades in Art and PE. He could go on the 'A' level courses he wanted. Most of his crew had done well, too. They were not quiet about it. They jumped in the air, shouted and swore. Gillian Newcombe embraced a weeping Alice Lawton, who had achieved eight grade 9s. As Miss Starr commented, "They're just as cuckoo as poor Lee Doonan!"

Later that morning, the new Executive Head, Ray Maxwell, joined Rhiannon and me to analyse the results. He was the Headteacher of Elm Forest, the Trust's most improved school in the region. He told Rhiannon he would operate as a line manager to both Acting Heads, Rhiannon and his former deputy at Elm Forest. He made it clear that he would have no compunction about intervening directly in the delivery of the Action Plan, should progress falter. He would observe, coach and monitor staff. And he would lead the pupil mentoring.

Ray was in many ways the ideal choice for the job. In his eight years at Elm Forest, he had transformed the school from an underachieving rural backwater to a magnet for aspiring families from all over Holmesside. Like Rhiannon, his first degree was in politics and he had the measure of the Local Authority Officers and the Trustees. He had a reputation for ruthlessness with Elm Forest staff but beneath the tough Geordie veneer, there was a touching humility. He was someone with a lot of answers who still wanted to learn. I had never met a Head who cared more about eradicating educational failure.

By the time the new academic year began, a tall metal fence ringed the New Eydon. The builders' materials had been cleared and trees planted. There was a garden with chrysanthemums in full flower in the forecourt. All signs of the industrial site from which it had arisen had been erased. The new building's gently curving walls were sheathed in green-tinged copper shingles. The main entrance was designed to impress, a vast atrium, three storeys tall. This would be a cathedral to learning: waste ground no longer.

The interior design with its trees, stone garden and running water gave an air of tranquillity. Around the ground floor, Miss Starr had arranged life-sized photographs of the last year's leavers, snapped at the moment they opened their GCSE letters. Not all of them were flattering, but they captured the crazy reality of that day. Under each picture was a sober list of that pupil's achievements and destination. On the first floor, next to my study, there was a parallel gallery of all the staff. The veterans amongst them had quotations from the former pupils, thanking them for all the help and support they had given.

Rhiannon gave the welcoming address to the staff when we returned to school. She described the building works that had taken place over the holiday. She thanked the staff as a whole for their hard work with the Year 11 pupils. And she read the stories about the exam results and Noha's medal from the local papers. Employing a mountaineering analogy, Rhiannon said it may feel like we were at the top of a cliff, but there was still a big new overhang we would have to climb. What the children needed above all was more settled teaching. Our biggest challenge was to reduce the rates of staff turnover.

Ray Maxwell spoke next. He gave an astute overview, commending Eydon Vale's results and the effects of the building work in giving us a fresh start. Speaking to the established staff, he said he had been all too well aware of the turmoil that "special measures" had generated. But this had led to some remarkable changes. For these to continue, we had to plan even greater collaboration between Elm Forest and the New Eydon.

Ray gave us a brief taste of his philosophy of education. He believed that teachers who became Ofsted Inspectors, education consultants or lecturers quickly lost the feel for what works in classes. As their knowledge lost its classroom roots, their credibility with teachers evaporated. He argued that partnerships between working teachers were at least as important as in-service training by outside experts.

My role that morning was to be product champion for Guided Discipline. In the previous two terms, we had devoted 14 hours of staff training to it. The new staff could probably manage with slightly less, given what HMI Megat had told us about the "dramatic" improvement in our pupils' behaviour.

From the investigations that had been carried out by the researchers from Sheffield University in the Summer Term, it was clear that our biggest problem was not with the children who had psychological problems, but with those who had internalised anti-social norms. They had told us that while the great majority of pupils supported our strategy, there was a group of troublemakers who were still frankly mutinous. The children differentiated between "the headbangers" and "the smokers". Our focus should be on "the smokers".

"Over the last few years, these troublemakers had learned how to argue back, get away with the minimum in class and avoid homework. Some specialised in non-stop petty disruption, but a lot just swore under their breath, grumbled, sulked and spent break times smoking dope. They held up our teaching," I emphasised.

"These children were so irritating, we were falling into the trap of repaying their negative behaviour with sanctions This was just perpetuating a vicious cycle. We needed to keep catching all our students when they did something good: recognising and supporting them whenever they behaved appropriately and letting them know we liked them, day in and day out."

Everyone on the staff had to keep signing the planners and giving out chocolate bars every lesson. We had to be explicit and use the whole rigmarole of praise; keep repeating "Excellent start, Johnny" and "You are working nicely, Chardonnay", as well as sending letters and making phone calls home. Above all, we had to ensure that children who had habitually disrupted their lessons previously were not excluded from the praise. They had to get their fair share of positive reinforcement.

This brief introduction was followed up the next day with a further three hours of practical skills training for the new staff. We emphasised that we had to keep moving forward, raising the standards every term. We played the Guided Discipline training videos and kept pausing them to emphasise key strategies like the broken record technique. Experience had taught us how well this had worked with even our most disenchanted students, even in unstructured situations.

When they returned from the long summer holiday, the pupils looked quite different. The weather had been hot and sunny all over Europe and North America. In some areas, this had led to droughts, in others forest fires. As they sat in their opening assemblies, the children looked tanned, healthy and calm. I told them it felt as if a terrible firestorm had passed over the New Eydon.

Staff who had been at Eydon Vale could not believe how quietly the new term had begun. The school had been eerily calm. No pupils were wandering the corridors. The vast majority of the children seem much more settled. "It's like I'm in a sci-fi film. I've gone through a portal into a new dimension," one PE teacher commented.

"Yeah, right," said Kylie Lawrence sourly. "What could possibly go wrong?"

At that moment, the new fire alarms went off. A minor accident as the cooks were preparing the day's stew had triggered the kitchens' smoke detectors. Even though there had been no fire practices for two terms, the teachers and children filed out and assembled calmly in the old playground behind the new school.

"Thor" Thurwell, a gloomy, old, technology teacher, whose droll humour always reminded me of Hamlet's gravedigger, assured the new staff, "The last time Eydon Vale had a fire practice, a hundred children jumped over the back fence and ran off for the day." He had been among the sceptics of Guided Discipline. He mourned the loss of traditional craft skills and had always relied on the sense of menace to maintain order. The story went that he had earned his nickname by throwing a hammer at a pupil who was not listening to him.

The 14 newly arrived teachers had a slightly different perspective to the established staff. One of the major barriers to improving the quality of teaching in the months that followed the original HMI Inspection had been the long-term absence of six of the Heads of Department. When the school had been placed in special measures, it lacked Heads of English, Maths, Science, ICT and Humanities. Like the former SENCo, who had found a job in the south-west as a Local Authority Adviser and Ofsted Inspector for Special Needs, these had now been replaced.

We had two major worries. There was a danger that some of the new staff might drop out in the first week. Our other concern was that if one or two of the established staff went off sick in the first fortnight, this might start an avalanche. Elizabeth Oliphant, the long-standing and brilliant Head of Art, had to go home with stress symptoms on the second day. However, Joan Lafresne, the wife of our photography teacher, came in to cover her lessons. Joan had years of experience of teaching Business Studies in a Further Education College. When the Head of Art returned from sick leave, they team-taught for a fortnight. Joan then took on a post in the ICT Department.

Maria Telemann, a probationary History teacher sent to us by a supply agency, cast a spell over her pupils. She had started the Year 8 lesson I happened to observe with a brief film clip about the causes of the English Civil War. Then she had given out sets of source materials about the moment when the King heard his Queen would be impeached. She had divided the pupils into two groups. Half had to write short speeches as MPs and half as King Charles' courtiers. The moment she wanted the class to focus on was Charles' decision to arrest the five leading dissenters.

She demonstrated how the pupils could adapt the sources and turn them into theatre. They incorporated their speeches into simple scripts, which they rehearsed in small groups. Lastly, she picked out the most competent children to improvise the drama under her direction. Just as I entered the classroom, a boy with a cardboard crown on his head was confronting the Speaker. "I see the birds have flown!" he declared magnificently.

On the first Friday evening of the term, a delegation from that Year 8 class rushed up and exclaimed, "We've just had Miss Telemann again!"

"She makes us all stand and say, 'Good morning, respected teacher!' before the lesson."

"Then she replies, 'Good morning, respected pupils!'," said another.

"She's our favourite teacher, but she says she's leaving. Can't you change her mind?"

Miss Telemann herself had just been offered another supply job in an outstanding school. But I caught her just as she was getting into her car that evening and told her what the children thought of her. So, she agreed to stay for one more week. What prompted her to continue after that was the arrival of two lively young Australian teachers.

"Whiz" Wilson and Claire Penny had both been attracted to the New Eydon because of its superior sporting facilities. Whiz played Minor League cricket and taught Geography. They were both broad-minded, skilled and assertive teachers, and had few problems managing the pupils, but they found the lack of team spirit puzzling. It seemed to take so much more energy for them to motivate pupils. Individuals like Noha were keen but many others refused to bring their PE kit, week after week, preferring to sit out the lessons on the touchline. Far fewer of our pupils enjoyed sport compared to those they had left behind in Australia.

There was no doubt that an increasing minority of children were happy in school, however. On the way to their after-school Master Class in Science, two clever Year 11 pupils, Nicole and Kayleigh, showed a little of that enjoyment. When they thought the corridors were clear and no one was watching, they did an impromptu tap-dance, collapsing into giggles. The staff at Eydon Vale had become used to unhappy children doing mad things. Here, at last, was an instance of two children acting out of *joie de vivre.*

Eydon Vale had never hosted a Prize Giving Ceremony for the children who had done well in the exams, so I suggested we should ask Jacob Hornsby if we could hold one in the lovely Georgian building at the heart of his Sixth Form College. Rhiannon invited her old politics professor to give the keynote address. A member of the Sutton Trust, he took a particular interest in schemes that would encourage children from deprived areas to apply to university.

"You are the most intelligent generation ever born on this planet," the Professor told the audience. "One hundred years ago, when Alfred Binet invented IQ tests, most English children left school at 12. Average class sizes were 42. Only 4 per cent took school exams. When Binet retested pupils ten years later, the proportion with above average IQ scores had gone up. We have kept resetting the average every ten years for most of the last century. If we gave out the original IQ tests now, three-quarters of you would be above the old average. You are smarter than your parents..."

In the pause, tittering went around the atrium. The Professor then added the punchline, "And they are brighter than your grandparents. The average pay for teachers is four times higher than it was when inflation is considered. That is because a well-educated workforce matters more and more these days. It's no good just learning to read and write copperplate as children did 100 years ago. In these days of computers and automation, everyone will need to keep studying far longer just to get a job.

"I like to think of education as a corridor. It has doors leading off it at regular intervals. The further down the educational corridor we go, the more doors are open to us. And every year that corridor gets longer. Half a century ago, my mother was living on a council estate not far from here. She had passed the 11+ and went to the Grammar School. Her ambition was to become a doctor, but her careers advisor told her that girls like her would be much happier as nurses. He was the Deputy Head, and she believed him. It wasn't until she was in her fifties that she realised her dream of taking a degree."

As he looked around the hall, there were plenty of mothers nodding their heads at their daughters. "There was a 'poverty of expectations', not just in our family but in the country as a whole. It was the norm for the best opportunities, like jobs in the top professions, to be reserved for boys from the most privileged families. And that was that. But since then, things have begun to improve. When I was your age, only one in six pupils went on to Higher Education. Nowadays, just over half of all 18-year olds do.

"Many schools and their pupils are starting to aim a lot higher. As a nation, we can't afford for you to get left behind. I know that student loans must be putting some of you off university. Starting on a career with big debts takes courage, especially if your parents are not in a position to help you out. But in the long term, you will see the benefits. From all I hear, Eydon Vale's pupils worked incredibly hard in their last two terms. All I can say is keep it up."

After he had distributed the awards, three pupils from my old English group came to the front of the stage and told the parents about the results that they and their friends got at GCSE. They explained precisely how hard they had had to work in Year 11 and how much support they had had from the staff. Alice Lawton spoke about the sense of failure she had felt just nine months before. "Just because you go to a failing school, it doesn't mean you have to be a failure. Right?"

At the end of the evening, her mother came over to me and expostulated about the awards to staff that ended the evening. "Miss Starr, Mr Smithson and the Head of Year were all given bottles of champagne. Even Miss Starr's PA got a bunch of flowers. None of them came in for the after-school lessons. You were completely disrespected!"

* * *

I was a little nonplussed when Ray Maxwell proposed a uniform purge as his first initiative. In my experience, they never made much difference to pupil learning, but he believed that this could empower the staff. In the fortnight before, we reminded the pupils of what they ought to wear to school. By then, very few were breaking the main rules about shirts, sweatshirts, skirts and trousers, but there were about 20 of the "smokers" in each year who sported white trainers instead of black shoes.

Ray said he would send home any child in Years 9-11 who arrived at school out of uniform. Younger pupils would be put in isolation. There were staff, particularly among the Year Tutors, who worried what would happen if a child sent home to change was injured in a road accident. Rhiannon had sent a letter warning the parents and I visited every classroom in the school on the Friday afternoon before the purge, emphasising our seriousness.

Ray had locked all the alternative school entrances first thing on the Monday morning. As the children filed in the main entry, they were met by half a dozen stony-faced members of the Senior Management and Pastoral Teams. On the first day, 46 pupils who were not wearing uniform were sent home to change, but the next day, there were only three. As it became clear that we were serious, though, there was a change of heart, both among the pupils and staff. Led by Rhiannon, the gatekeepers became greeters, bidding the children a nice day individually and by name.

By chance, a Health and Safety Inspector happened to come round the school the week of the purge. He had had a rather disturbing experience on his annual visit the previous September. As he had arrived, a supply teacher burst into the foyer, threw his keys on the receptionist's desk and said, "Right, that's it! I've had enough. I'm leaving."

As the Health and Safety Inspector was conducted down the corridor the previous time, the noise and the crush of children had overwhelmed him, and he had asked to leave. As I took him from class to class now, he had kept repeating, "This is remarkable! And all the children in *this* class are in uniform.... This is amazing! All the children in *this* class are in uniform, too!" He was astonished at the transformation.

Many staff seemed to agree that Ray's purge and his additional presence on the corridors had made the children even more manageable. This was borne out by our statistics. The tally of serious causes for concern per week had dropped from 191 by the time of June's HMI visit to 140 per week in the new term, but in the week after the November half term, we recorded only 74. The distribution of the points on a graph resembled the curve of radioactive decay.

In the week before the October half-term break, the pupils and staff at the New Eydon seemed to start smiling again and there were only a few reminders of the bad, old days. Most children were beginning to experience whole days of at least satisfactory teaching and learning. A long-term supply teacher of Food Studies, whose first lessons in the previous April had been devastated by children throwing eggs and flour at her, was heartened by what she now saw. As she said, her lessons were beginning to *smell like Christmas.*

Ray Maxwell plunged into his new role of Chief Executive with zeal. Following the uniform purge, the second item on Ray's agenda was the evaluation of teaching and learning. Having observed every member of staff teaching twice a week through September and October, I estimated that about 85% of lessons across the curriculum were now at least satisfactory. Most of the teachers whose work was still unsatisfactory were long-term supply staff. Christian Dean agreed, though he pointed out that when HMI returned in November, they would just be looking at the three core subjects: English, Maths and Science, plus ICT. Here the figures were slightly lower.

For Ray, this was an issue that needed to be confronted. He told Rhiannon she should curtail her external meetings. They were going to carry out an observation schedule and he wanted the four key departments to follow this up with a programme of self-evaluation. He planned to bring along the latest set of Ofsted's self-evaluation sheets to the next middle managers' meeting.

Ray wanted to give all senior and middle management the authority to challenge under-achieving teachers directly. The first whole lesson classroom observation that Ray carried out was of the deputy head in the English Department. He judged Gilly Johnson, an experienced and popular member of staff, unsatisfactory. Until then, her Ofsted and HMI grades had always been good. She complained that she had been given insufficient time to prepare, but Ray was not to be deflected.

Ray and I had got into the habit of dropping into each other's offices when we arrived in the morning. For most of my career in Special Needs, it had easier for me to talk to women than men. But with John Silver at Rectory Road and now with Ray Maxwell, there was a sense we could be open and honest with one another. John had been a boxer and I had learned never to pull figurative punches with him. It was the same with Ray. I queried the value of such negative feedback. In answer, he reminded me that he would be asking no more of the staff than the HMI would.

For his part, Ray questioned whether we still needed to use chocolate bars as tangible rewards. Many more pupils were beginning to enjoy learning for its own sake. Instead of the constant wandering around, pushing, poking, fidgeting and chattering that had characterized their behaviour such a short time before, more classes were attentive for increasingly lengthy periods. They listened to one another and liked what they heard. As I entered Angela Clayton's Year 11 English class, I heard one of the pupils say, "Sometimes I'm amazed by the words that come out of my mouth. I'm normally so shy."

The next inspection was much less stressful: the verdict that we had made "progress to be proud of." The greatest improvement had been once again in the areas of pupil behaviour and attitudes. Relationships between adults and children were now seen as "warm and respectful". HMI Salomon judged that the best behaviour occurred in those lessons where pupils felt the teachers were working hard, that they had prepared their lessons properly and they were being set demanding work. The great majority of pupils were seen as "enthusiastic" about the changes in the school and "very willing to help". They were becoming confident enough to ask where they did not understand and eager to share their work.

While the whole school training in Guided Discipline would have to continue, more attention would be focused on the least assertive teachers. It was as if this small group were constantly on edge, expecting all the old problems to recur. HMI's verdict on Ray Maxwell's reforms was that there was now a "rigorous policy on uniform and swearing", but that the school management still had some way to go to ensure that the weaker staff "did not back off". HMI had also observed some "boisterous behaviour in unstructured situations".

HMI's other main criticisms were reserved for attendance and exclusions, but overall, they thought leadership and management were "strong and determined". The amount of mentoring that Rhiannon required as an Acting Head, was now decreasing. Her management style was seen as "appropriately robust". She "exuded confidence" in the New Eydon's ability to improve. She had a "sensible view of what could be achieved in a short amount of time" and the school was "taking the right size of bites to continue making progress".

On the back of these findings, the Trust advertised the Headship of the New Eydon. Rhiannon had always cut an impressive figure with inspectors, officers and Trustees. They were content for the interviews to go ahead, even though she was the only applicant. The process was completed within a couple of hours and her appointment was confirmed by the school's governors that same evening.

Chapter Fifteen: Christmas Concert

The Assistant Heads, whom Rhiannon had appointed in the summer term, were full of energy and determination. Milo O'Donnell was the more extrovert. His towering forehead, gaunt cheekbones and Van Dyke beard were on the front pages of national newspapers by the end of the year. He taught English. Peter McIntosh was prematurely bald, tall and wiry. He was the new Head of Maths and had been hired to write the next year's school timetable.

Milo could undoubtedly be implacable when required, but for most of the time, he was witty and personable. He picked up new ideas quickly and communicated them easily. As Head of English and Drama at his last school, he had created a poetry club and produced the school play, but according to his reference, he had also "ruthlessly transformed" his department's exam results. He was still in his 20s, very young for such a promotion. His head was completely shaven, and he always wore his tie loose under his waistcoat, giving him a deceptively casual air.

At the end of that Christmas term, my wife and I invited him and his partner for Sunday lunch. In the afternoon, we went out for a walk in the woods behind our house. Milo grilled me about Ray Maxwell's plans., then told me about the novel he was writing with Kev Samson, Elroy's little brother. Even though I thought I knew Elroy and had heard Kev's ghost story, I had little understanding of how tragic their lives had been. Apparently, the family had had to "do a flit" from London to Holmesside to escape Mrs Samson's abusive husband.

They had only been living in Holmesside for ten days when Kev's dad came round. It had not taken him long to find out where they lived. He banged on the door and told them to let him in. His mum replied she was ringing the police, but this was no deterrent. Kev's dad punched in the glass and opened the latch. Kev had told Milo he stood in the doorway "snorting like a bull". There was blood running down his arm. He was just like the monster that Kev had seen in a recurrent nightmare.

Elroy faced up to him. He had learned to box at a Youth Centre in London but all he had to fend off his father was a kitchen stool. Just then, the phone rang. Kev picked up the phone. It was Mrs Blake, his teacher from the Special Unit. Kev had told Mrs Blake his dad had broken in. "Can you get the police?" he asked.

At that, Kev's dad saw red. He went for Kev's mum. Elroy kept smashing the stool into his dad's back, but it had little effect. His dad was drunk and did not seem to feel the pain. He just kept hitting Kev's mum.

Nothing else could stop him, so Kev jumped on his dad's back. He used to jump up like this when he was little. His dad used to give him a piggyback. Kev got his arm around his dad's neck, but his dad was not playing now. He bucked his head and banged Kev against the wall, making Kev bite his tongue.

There was always a police van on the estate where the Samsons lived. Kev could hear the siren and see the blue lights. There were two PCs: a man and a woman. They let themselves in the house and drew their batons. Elroy and Kev held onto their dad. The police wrestled him to the ground. They twisted his arms behind his back. The cuffs went on. His dad was led away shouting, "You have not seen the last of me."

The police were saying, "You do not have to say anything...." That was the last time Kev or Elroy saw their dad. It was two in the morning before they had had their door boarded up, washed the blood off the carpet and tidied the front room.

The family were all sitting around with cups of tea when the doorbell rang again. The same woman constable was outside. "Can I come in?" she asked. "It's bad news, I'm afraid."

She sat next to Kev's mum. She told them Kev's dad was dead. "He may have had some matches. He set fire to himself in the cells. By the time we got to him, it was too late. There will be a full inquiry."

Elroy and their mother wanted to move back to London after that, but Kev was adamant he wanted to stay at the special unit in Eydon Vale. "I hated my old special school. Mrs Blake is the best teacher I've ever had. She knows how to calm me down. She wanted to have a chat with my mum to tell her how well I was getting on with my reading the night dad came round. That's why she rang up."

After they went back to school, Kev seemed to be enjoying lessons and keeping out of trouble. Inside, though, he was feeling increasingly anxious and depressed. He did not tell anyone, but he had started seeing his dad again. First, he kept seeing his dad's face in the pattern of the carpet. Then he saw it on the face of next door's cat. Then he caught sight of his dad's old yellow and green tee shirt in a crowd. And as he was walking into school one morning, he heard his voice.

Kev did not want to tell his mum. She had so much to deal with. He had to sort himself out. So, he started going out for a run in the woods outside Holmesside – often with his new friend Noha. And that was where he met his dad's ghost. According to Kev, "There was a big yellow moon. It was just coming up. Its light fell on the path. It was almost as bright as day. And then his dad was there. He stood in the pathway filling it up. He had not shaved. He had a scraggly beard and his old tee shirt. He looked just the same as the day he died.

"I'm sorry, son," a voice said. It was just like his dad's growly voice. He held out his arms to Kev. It was like he wanted Kev to run into them, but Kev kept his distance. His dad just stood there in the moonlight. "I let you down, son. But you are not to let yourself down."

Tears came into Kev's eyes. When he brushed them away, his dad's ghost was gone. There were only a few of last year's leaves on the beech trees, and all he could hear was a little rattling in the breeze. Kev was not afraid. If anything, he felt relieved. According to Milo, it was as if a pact had been made between them. There was nothing more to be said.

Kev did not tell his mum or Elroy about the appearance of his dad's ghost, but one day, when they were alone, Mrs Blake asked him how he was coping. Kev told her the whole story. He was a good ghost, she told Kev. "He told you not to let yourself down, didn't he?" Mrs Blake had asked him which of his mainstream teachers could help him fulfil this pact he had made with his father. So, that's why Kev asked Milo to help him with his writing. It was only one lesson a week, but he had learned more from Kev about the life of the New Eydon's pupils than he had taught Kev.

"Teaching Kev has been like a peak experience. Do you know what I mean?" Milo asked me.

"Don't go breaking his heart," I told him, echoing the warning Mrs Lawton gave me when her daughter Alice's English started to take wing a little under a year previously.

That Christmas Term finished with the Year 11 mock GCSE exams and a benefit concert. Milo played a decent guitar. He got together with Peter McIntosh and John Sugar from the PE department to play Oasis covers. The pupils in Peter's Maths classes were amazed. His teaching style was that of a martinet. He relied more on sanctions than praise and was always nagging them to be silent. That lunchtime they saw another side of him. As they danced along, they rolled their eyes in mock admiration. As one of the lunchtime supervisors commented, "This will do wonders for his street cred!"

Their set was a great success. Everyone joined in their rendition of the Manchester anthem: 'Don't look back in anger'. Nicole and Kayleigh, the two girls I had caught practising their tap-dancing on the way to Science, donned Abba wigs and sang classics like 'Thank You for the Music'. Groups of younger pupils sang, danced and rode unicycles around the atrium. Pandora O'Connell, a gravelly-voiced comedienne from Year 11, acted as compère.

In the end, Father Christmas came onto the stage, juggling four, then five, then six silver balls. As he reached the climax of his act, he tore off his Santa wig and full, white beard, revealing Dr Adam Awad. "Give generously," he bellowed to cheers and whistles. I had asked him to finish off the concert with a few words about the collapse of the Syrian Health Service and the courageous work of the Red Cross, many of whose staff were being killed on the front line.

As soon as the limelight fell on Adam, the talking stopped. Everyone listened. It was the first time since he had left his job as a vice principal that he had had a whole school's attention. Buckets were passed around and the prefects collected over £150 from these poor children and their teachers.

The thought passed through my mind, that if I had to retire in another five years, there were so many talented staff the school could call on to take my place.

Chapter 16: Snowstorm

There were no New Year blues when staff and pupils returned to The New Eydon after the Christmas holidays. Indeed, the mood was reminiscent of the start of the Easter Term a year previously, when both adults and pupils had been so ready for a change. On the first day of the new Easter Term, The New Eydon was closed for a teachers' training day, just as it had been the previous year. We needed to review our Guided Discipline Programme and our Teaching Plans.

Rhiannon welcomed the staff. She explained that she and Ray Maxwell had agreed to extend Elm Forest's House System to our school. We were going to use house points as yet another way of boosting pupils' confidence and reinforcing positive classroom behaviour. We had started the previous year with tracking sheets, as a way of noting praise and warnings. We were now going to use them to record House points as well.

Her first Assistant Head, Brian Smithson, explained that the main issue facing us was the need to lower the number of recorded external fixed-term exclusions whilst simultaneously raising standards of behaviour. In the previous year, we had made the mistake of re-excluding the same pupils for brief periods. Each of these suspensions had been counted against us. He proposed that excluded pupils be put out for much longer periods, and the disciplinary committee of the Governing Body would only readmit them to mainstream lessons after a further period of "internal isolation".

Ray Maxwell, the Chief Executive, started our review of disciplinary procedures with a reminder of what the school council had told me about the corridors. They wanted a heavier adult presence. At the most recent parents' forum, we had had a show of hands. Some thought we were still too soft, an equal number that we were too strict. But there had been support for more purges, and the parents wanted more staff on the corridors. I then took the staff through the next stage of our Guided Discipline training programme. I opened with an essay one of the Year 9 pupils had written the previous term:

When I first started this school, there was no discipline. We all did what we liked. That's why some people are cocky and big-headed now. People would pick on each other or call each other names and nothing would be done about it. In lots of lessons, no one paid attention to the teacher. Discipline is not so bad now. Lessons are better, the teachers are stricter and now we get to learn. But it still needs to be improved. There are still a few people who need to satisfy their egos by disrupting. Things only calm down when they are taken out by the on-call tutor and put in internal isolation.

Reinforcing positive behaviour had provided the real engine of change over the last 12 months. But we also had lots of experts now in the school who knew how to use eye contact or a quiet word to redirect non-disruptive behaviour before it escalated. There was a microsecond when the pupils glanced at teachers and had to make up their minds about how serious we were. Every time we looked away or raised our voices at that crucial moment, we would lose ground.

I reassured the staff that virtually all the pupils knew what to expect when they entered the classroom. We had trained the great majority of children how to come in, get out their homework and equipment, raise their hands and fall silent when they had completed a practical task. Such routines were not universal, though, and such inconsistency may have been inhibiting further progress in learning. Pupils from failing schools needed even more consistency and firmer boundaries than those in more settled areas. Predictable routines would help to create the virtuous circle of less disruption, more adventurous teaching and higher levels of pupil participation.

Ray Maxwell wound up the day with a summary of the changes that had come about in the latest Ofsted framework. The Department of Education had given Ray the latest progress charts for both The New Eydon and Elm Forest. These gave us detailed information about which pupils had done well and which were underachieving, subject by subject, class by class. The data made clear precisely how much progress the targeted New Eydon pupils had made in their last six months. He was going to ask for volunteers to repeat last year's after-school lessons and Saturday School.

Ray summoned a meeting during the regular Year 11 parents' evening to underline the importance of these sessions. In the letter of invitation, he also told them the good news about our latest value-added grades in the league tables. The New Eydon had moved from bottom of the Holmesside table to the middle, thanks mainly to these sessions.

There was an excellent turnout to the first of the new term's after-school classes and 53 of the targeted children arrived on time for the start of my first Saturday morning session. After a quick breakfast of freshly baked croissants and a brief introduction from me, they wrote a descriptive essay under exam conditions about the most memorable time in their lives.

The best piece described a family holiday in Devon, in which each paragraph finished with an understated paean to each member of the writer's family. The real drama came in the pupil's concluding section. Immediately after the holiday, the writer's mother had left home, so that this brief holiday turned out to have been the last time the family had spent together.

A couple of Saturdays later, Ray telephoned me at home with the news that Ofsted would be inspecting Elm Forest the following week. By chance there was a heavy snowstorm on the Tuesday night of Elm Forest's Inspection and another band of snow and high winds was forecast for later that day. With Ray Maxwell out of contact because of the Inspection, Rhiannon telephoned me at 6:30 on that Wednesday morning to discuss the weather. She was concerned about the number of teachers who had to drive in on country roads. If insufficient numbers came in, she worried it might be difficult for us to maintain effective discipline. She asked my advice about closing the school.

Her decision to keep the New Eydon open seemed justified in the event, as only four teachers called in snowbound. Four more arrived 20 minutes late, but we managed to cover all their classes. In the pre-school briefing, Brian Smithson repeated our rule that the children were only allowed to throw snowballs on the basketball courts.

As I left the staffroom, Peter McIntosh, the Head of Maths and the second Assistant Deputy Headteacher muttered nervously that 70 pupils were snowballing in the main playground. As soon as Brian and I appeared, they went into lessons. I caught six with snowballs in their hands and sent them to Brian's office for exclusion. At the change of lessons later that morning, a group of 40 Year 11 pupils ran around the front of the building, snowballing each other. Showing great determination and courage, Thor Thurwell, the asthmatic, 60-year-old Technology teacher, ran outside and made them return to lessons.

During the morning break, most of the children went snowballing in the basketball courts as they were allowed, but a lot took our advice and sheltered on the corridors or in the tuck shop. A couple of Year 7 pupils came in from the basketball courts crying, but none had been injured. They thought it would be fun to play in the snow, but had not realised how heavy-handed the older New Eydon pupils could be. To their credit, a lot of staff went outside at break and the children came in peaceably. According to the Duty Tutor, the school was quiet next lesson. I felt it would be safe to carry on team teaching the Magic Carpet lessons with a bottom set Year 7 English class.

At about midday, we had a tremendous blizzard. Suddenly the classroom went dark. At the beginning of lunch, some older pupils started snowballing the lunch queues in the main playground, but this tailed off. Without asking my advice or that of her Year Tutors, she decided to cancel afternoon school. Rhiannon decided to call a couple of lunchtime assemblies, one led by Brian Smithson and Peter McIntosh, the other by her. When I heard of her plan, I was seriously alarmed. Why hold assemblies? Was she trying to prove her credentials as New Eydon's headteacher in Ray's absence? We had never carried out a health and safety review of this procedure and I seriously doubted she could carry it out in an orderly manner.

After lunchtime registration, a message was sent around the school that all the pupils should muster in the two halls: the two older year groups in the assembly room with Brian Smithson, the three younger ones with her in the dining hall. This meant there would be 200 more children in the dining hall than the fire regulations permitted. The caretakers had had insufficient time to clear the heavy, new dining tables after lunch, so there would be even less room for the pupils to manoeuvre.

One of the Heads of Year banged on a table for silence, but Rhiannon started addressing the pupils while many of them were still chattering. Kate Bullamore, the teacher who had earlier confessed to "vertigo", put her hand on my arm and looked me in the eye. She was beseeching me to bring the children to order so Rhiannon could make herself heard.

Kate had seen Rhiannon teaching when she had first come to Eydon Vale as a Deputy Head. She knew how hard Rhiannon had found it to establish herself and how little classroom contact she had had since then. If Rhiannon could not make a class listen to her, what chance did she have with such a large number? Kate and I knew how much Rhiannon would hate this. She would presume that I was undermining her authority as Headteacher. But we were in a potentially dangerous situation.

After I shouted the pupils down, Rhiannon said that those who had no one at home should stay in school. Those who had mobile phones could use them when the Assembly was over. Then she asked the pupils at the front of the Hall to leave in an orderly fashion. Many of the pupils had been unable to hear her. As the front rows started to move towards the door, there was a surge from the back. What followed reminded me of the mobbing behaviour I thought we had extinguished 12 months before. At least 100 pupils rushed the door. Some of the smaller ones were thrown to the floor. A 14-year-old caught in the crush broke her arm. The racket was appalling. This was a riot.

Peter McIntosh's management of the younger pupils was much more successful. With the help of the Heads of Year, he managed to get them to file out of the dining hall in an orderly manner. As I stood at the main gates seeing the pupils off-site, a group of older boys remained behind. They ambushed Peter at the exit door. They chucked snowballs and blocks of ice at him and bundled him into a snowdrift. His coat and hair were drenched and when I saw him, he looked deeply shaken. He offered Rhiannon his resignation and went on intermittent sick leave. At the end of the year, he was to take up a post as a basic-scale Maths teacher in the Australian Outback.

Even though she was physically unscathed, Miss Starr appeared - if anything - even more shocked. When I dropped into the school secretariat on my way home, she was in a foetal position in the Office Manager's chair, white-faced and speechless. She could not look anyone in the face. She had lost all authority, and all the adults in the room knew it. There was no attempt to console her. I felt so deeply ashamed for her that I fleetingly considered tendering my resignation.

On their way out of school, the pupils' behaviour deteriorated even further. We had no idea what had been going on at the time, but the next day, the local police came in with several complaints about snowballs being thrown at neighbours and the traffic. A lorry had had to swerve when its windscreen was blocked and the pupils waiting at a nearby bus stop had narrowly escaped being run over.

The Office Manager openly speculated that if HMI had happened to visit The New Eydon that afternoon, they would have closed the school.

The incident with the Head of Maths took place outside her office, and she gave us the names of seven Year 11 pupils. Rhiannon was not in school until much later the next morning, so I took the reins. I telephoned the parents of the seven and told them on my own initiative that they would be given long, possibly permanent suspensions for assaulting a teacher. Other unknown Year 9 pupils had also been involved but there was not enough time to find out their names.

My priority was to send out a clear message about boundaries to all the year groups. I warned the pupils that as a school in special measures, we could not afford such dangerous behaviour. The excluded pupils included some of the most able GCSE students and in sending them home, we were risking their exam results. But we had to ensure the whole school understood the situation. No one was above the rules and such behaviour could not be tolerated. I spent the rest of the morning, touring every classroom, talking to pupils and staff in small groups and reinforcing that simple message. I suspected Rhiannon would think I was undermining her authority, but someone had to take the school in hand.

Half the staff judged the pupils' behaviour "a moment of madness". Others saw this whole episode as "an own goal". No one openly accused Miss Starr of letting us down, but plenty agreed with Thor Thurwell when he said, "We are back to square one. Eydon Vale had made 100 steps forward in the previous year. But in half an hour on that Tuesday afternoon, the New Eydon went back 99. Whatever have we unleashed?"

Attendance fell to 65%, and those pupils who did come in on Thursday looked anxious and ashamed. When Rhiannon did eventually appear, she was bullish. She wanted to carry on as if nothing had happened. She accepted the exclusion of the seven Year 11s who had snowballed Peter McIntosh as a *fait accompli*. But she would not allow me to investigate which of the Year 9s were involved in this incident. And she would not let Ray Maxwell know what had occurred.

For the next two days, the atmosphere in the New Eydon was funereal. There was no presence on the entry doors and Rhiannon relaxed the rule that pupils out of uniform be sent home. On the Friday Eileen Butcher, a newly appointed Educational Psychologist, happened to be in The New Eydon on a planned visit to carry out lesson observations on Kev and a couple of other unit pupils. I warned her that in the aftermath of the snowstorm, she might encounter a few instances of chaotic behaviour. In the event, there were few signs of behavioural difficulties.

The art class to which I accompanied her was settled. Like most other teachers, Dr Awad had anticipated his lessons might be more turbulent than usual, so he had gone to great lengths in his lesson planning. His pupils were working on a still life project. I had divided the class into three groups and arranged a bowl of fruit in one area, a pot of early Narcissi in another and a jumble of machine parts in a third.

As the psychologist entered the room, Adam was holding forth with a book of Impressionist prints. He was showing the first group examples of still lives by Cezanne, Van Gogh and Seurat. He had primed a watercolour brush with dry poster paint and was demonstrating how the Impressionists might have recreated an impression of light on the surfaces of apples. He was praising all the pupils' efforts, using operant reinforcement even more enthusiastically than usual.

The rest of the class may have been unusually sombre, but Kev moved around the room purposefully, gathering materials for his piece. He downloaded Magritte's surreal picture of the man with an apple in front of his face, creating a template of the apple and its leaves, then cut it out a piece of paper. He then layered red and yellow stripes that looked like the colouring of a Cox's Orange Pippin and put a mirror behind the cut-out. As he finished, I interpreted the look he gave the psychologist as 'How do you like them apples?'

There was a meeting of the School Council scheduled for the Friday after the snowstorm. Pandora O'Connell, the gravely voiced compere at the Christmas concert, asked if they could put aside the published agenda and discuss Wednesday's events with Rhiannon and me. They told us about incidents neither of us had known until then. One of the Year 10 representatives had been at the bus stop where a driver had had to pull his lorry to an emergency stop.

"It was terrifying. It was one of those big Tarmac lorries: a 32 tonner. It mounted the kerb next to me. I thought it was never going to stop in time. It made contact with one of the old ladies in the queue, though luckily, she wasn't injured. The driver was in a right state. He was going to ring the police and have all the kids arrested," she said.

The pupils were blunt. They told Rhiannon just how badly planned her response to the day had been. It would have better to have kept the children in school until just before home time. Katie Lawton, Alice's younger sister, said the pupils should then have been dismissed one class at a time. Staff whose pupils had left should then have helped the senior managers shepherd the children away from the site in small groups. All the pupils caught snowballing in the yard should have been excluded.

Ray did not hear about what had happened until the end of school on Friday. When he telephoned me, he was still fired up about Elm Forest's successful inspection, but by the time he had arrived at the New Eydon on Monday morning, his mood was unforgiving. He and the Heads of Year stood at the door stony-faced and sent home every pupil who was out of uniform.

Even though Rhiannon told Monday's pre-school briefing that she took full responsibility for the poor evacuation procedures, it became clear that she had informed neither the Chair of Governors nor the Trustees of the full seriousness of these events. Ray felt obliged to make a report of these incidents himself to the Federation Board. In one of our pre-school briefings the following week, he made no secret of the fact that he was considering her suspension as Headteacher.

Rhiannon's actions in the immediate aftermath of the snow had also been insufficiently firm to settle the children. At a specially convened union meeting, a significant minority of teachers said they had begun to find difficulty managing the behaviour of normally settled classes again. Four teachers were assaulted. The dynamics of the situation had shifted: the old sense of incipient mutiny had returned.

Things came to a head on a Thursday morning for me, when I asked my second stream Year 11 class to write an essay comparing poems from the English Anthology. We had spent the first two weeks of term analysing the poems separately and writing extended essays on them. We had then discussed a revision matrix. I thought I had done everything possible to prepare them, but it proved too much for three boys and they baulked. For a few minutes, they refused even to put pen to paper.

Memories stirred of the way groups of disaffected pupils at the New Eydon had previously blocked teachers. It was only after a reminder of the rules and a warning that they settled to work. When I saw the three refusers at the end of the lesson, they were all shocked at what they had done. A fortnight after the riot, two pupils whom I had excluded for their part in snowballing the Head of Maths also rejoined my class. This was the day I was to give back the essays the *refuseniks* had written and there were nervous glances around the room.

In the event, some of the marks were lower than might have been expected, but most had got grades 6 or 7 and I congratulated the class. They had made extraordinary progress in the last three terms and tackled a question that was far tougher than anything they had done before. Then I invited general comments and questions on the last two weeks.

Tom had insisted, 'No matter what the so-called witnesses said, I never snowballed Mr McIntosh. I never touched him. I was just an innocent bystander. I never laid a finger on him. Sending me home really upset my Nan. It made her ill. I shall never forgive you." The biggest issue that the refusers raised was that it had been unfair for me to set *two* timed essays a week, the second on a Saturday morning.

For the next Saturday Master Class, a wide range of pupils from the top three English sets came into school to write a descriptive essay under exam conditions. The targeted pupils who had been suspended joined the refusers and they all did well, so I was able to make positive phone calls home. My classes returned to good order.

This was not immediately apparent elsewhere. In the weeks following the riot and the assaulting of the teachers that followed it, the staff's use of the rules of Guided Discipline faltered and many reported the reappearance of mutiny in their classes. Since November, when the Governors had made Rhiannon permanent Head, she had wanted to dictate her own disciplinary agenda. She confidently assumed she was above the rules that the staff had agreed.

Milo was particularly incensed about the example she was setting. As he emailed: "A few of our colleagues have been turning a blind eye to infringements of the rules. They are letting the kids sit in their lessons in non-uniform tops and allowing them to access their cell phones. This informal suspension of the rules in one lesson has a knock-on effect for the next teacher. It undermines the vast majority of staff, who are still trying to stick to what we all agreed.

"If Ofsted were to hear about the riot, they would be merciless. The leadership team ought to hold a weekend meeting to audit our progress. We need to check on the developments in teaching and learning and review the effects of the riot on behaviour. Then we must hold another staff training evening and reassert Guided Discipline. We all need to show our support for it at this point.'

Feeling I had no alternative, I emailed Rhiannon and Ray a Crisis Action Plan. Rhiannon and Ray held a long telephone discussion about it over the weekend and she agreed to accept it. Ray told me that my email had deeply offended her, though, and emphasised that I had been "sailing close to the wind". However, he also said that if she had turned down my crisis plan, he would have suspended her as Headteacher. Rhiannon duly excluded four of the Year 9 pupils and asked me to set up a further Guided Discipline training session with the LEA consultant.

The next time Christian Dean "happened to drop in", I consulted him about all this. The classroom and corridor observations he had made that day suggested that while there were still a few Year 9 pupils taking a more confrontational stance, there was little seriously wrong with the school. It had taken us four exhausting terms to calm those stormy waters. We were a turbulent school no longer.

The effects of the Crisis Action Plan were plain to see. Rhiannon had excluded four of the pupils who assaulted staff. The response to the Guided Discipline training had been positive and there had been a rapid improvement in the ethos of the school. Technically Eydon Vale had come out of Special Measures when the staff and pupils transferred to its new premises. So far as Christian Dean was concerned, we had now ticked all the boxes. "You have calmed the school," he told me as he was leaving for the last time.

"Until the children who experienced that chaos have left, we'll always have to be careful," I replied.

Aftermath

According to a recent report by Chief Inspector to the Parliamentary Public Accounts Committee, there are 500 "intractable" schools in England. None has ever had a "good" or "outstanding" report in 15 years. Many fail Ofsted Inspections, free themselves from special measures and fail again. Most are in immiserated, predominantly white working-class areas like Holmesside. Problems that other schools overcome can prove catastrophic. As Amanda Spielman confessed, "This is nothing short of a scandal and is a betrayal of children's futures."

At a meeting of the Federation Board just before the end of term, Ray reviewed the effects of the snowstorm. The older pupils had been immediately excluded. However, a failure to get to grips with the Year 9 miscreants had led to further deterioration in behaviour. He felt that the Crisis Action Plan *was* pulling the school back from the brink. Rhiannon told the Board that she accepted full responsibility. She admitted that she might have let New Eydon down. Buoyed, perhaps, by the news that the New Eydon was out of special measures, her tone was bullish, though.

The very next day, Ray got involved in a confrontation with the Year 9 miscreants who had escaped suspension. He had not been present when the rule about not invading a pupil's space had been agreed, and as a group of them pushed past their Year Tutor on the corridors, Ray had put an arm out to block their escape. Jake Sangster, the frankly mutinous, red-faced younger brother of Pete, who told me on my first visit to Eydon Vale that he liked the school the way it was, pushed him aside. Mrs Sangster claimed Ray had grabbed Jake.

Rhiannon and the Chair of Governors agreed that Ray should not be officially suspended but ordered to stay in his office until the matter was resolved. She had told me the same over the incident where Ian had falsely accused me of scratching his neck the previous year. The police investigations were concluded so rapidly that I returned to work the next working day, but Ray was not so lucky. He was ordered to keep away from the classrooms, off the corridors and out of the playground for the whole of the summer term.

Hanif Megat's gnomic prophecy came back to me. Perhaps those months of exhausting hard work were making me paranoid, but I could not help feeling that now Ray had been ejected from the cockpit,

Rhiannon would try the same with me. On the last day of the Easter term, Rhiannon informed me of a complaint by the parent of a Year 9 boy. I had sent Jonathon home after seeing him throw a bottle across the playground. At his return to school interview with Rhiannon, he and his mother denied any involvement. So, I invited his mother into the school to see if we could resolve the matter. I asked Jonathon to tell his mother the truth, fixing him with what the pupils called my "death stare".

Jonathon burst into tears and confessed that he had lied to Rhiannon and her. The mother was shaken, even though I spoke in the quietest of voices. Rhiannon was waiting in the foyer just outside my room. There was no question that Jonathan had lied or that he had shown any remorse for defying the Headteacher. On their way out of school, Rhiannon promised his mother there would be a further investigation after the holiday.

That Easter our family went to Hawkshead with my old Daventry friend, Gordon Potts, for a week. At Esthwaite, just south of the town, there was a trout lake with boats for hire. Gordon, his wife and my wife walked around it, while I rowed out for some fly fishing. At the end of a fruitless hour, I took my rowboat back to the jetty. The misstep I made next cost me my career. As I was getting out, I fell into deep water.

At first, my puffer jacket kept my head well above the surface, but the water was paralysingly cold and I was gradually sucked under. I knew I could drown, so I bellowed to the boatman for help. He could not hear me, though. Luckily, Gordon had seen the whole incident. He raced back around the lake and helped pull me out. It was a narrow escape. I had already inhaled some water and could easily have drowned.

I spent most of the rest of the week in bed. My temperature went up and breathing became more difficult. One moment I would be sweating, the next shivering. I had pains in my side and chest, especially when I was coughing. My head and limbs ached and on the morning that we went home, I brought up some blood. An appointment was arranged with my GP and she diagnosed pneumonia.

All through this time, I had a series of the most wonderful dreams. I was in the chapel of Kings College, Cambridge. Instead of choir stalls, the walls were lined with books. When I took these down and read them, they turned out to be the story of my life, told in the tiniest of detail. In my dream, I kept thinking, 'So this is what happened. Now it makes sense'. For a few moments when I awoke, I thought I understood every aspect of my life.

The details I forgot within half a minute. But my sense of an organising principle remained. The mitigation of educational failure – the theme that had dominated my career – became clearer to me than ever. I knew that for a significant minority of teachers, enabling illiterate, disabled, desperate or mutinous children to overcome their reluctance to learn was a privilege. I had a clear sense of the minimum that schools serving precarious communities need to flourish. Praise based behavioural strategies needed to be delivered. Rules must be clear. Ofsted had never been designed to help schools like Eydon Vale. Its effect on these communities was a scandal.

I was far too unwell to consider returning to school that term. My GP thought I might even be lucky to return to work by September. If I wished to ask for early retirement on the grounds of ill health, she would be happy to provide the evidence. I was stunned. Teaching had been my life. I understood more clearly than ever what the New Eydon needed to flourish. The children needed me.

In the six weeks following my sick leave, behaviour at the New Eydon rapidly deteriorated. A union meeting was called to discuss a motion of no confidence in Rhiannon's leadership. There were unreported assaults on staff. Teachers were sworn at and defied. The number of broken windows went up from less than five per week to 30, almost as high as when the previous Head had resigned. Even the glass in Rhiannon's door was smashed. After five weeks of supply teaching, pupils in my second set Year 10 lit a fire in the classroom

Milo tried to inject a sense of direction. In the absence of Ray and me, he went on playground duty every break and lunchtime and out on the school gates every night. He spotted Gerry Conlin's crew selling drugs. He was determined to confront them. When they saw him, Gerry and his gang ran away. Milo had not been appointed as Assistant Head when Bea Wright gave her lecture on physical threats. He acted unilaterally, sprinting after them on his own, without contacting the police or calling on the other duty teachers for backup.

Cornered in a nearby side street, Gerry pulled out a kitchen knife. Kev Samson, who happened to be walking that way home, saw the danger. He jumped on the aggressor's back, just as he did the night his father died. As Kev shouted, "Please stop", Gerry slashed at him, then stabbed Milo in the chest. The police and ambulance arrived within four minutes. Gerry was arrested shortly afterwards. Milo and Kev were taken away by the paramedics, both unconscious.

Dr Awad came round to my house to tell me what had happened. He had been in the art room clearing up after the last lesson when he heard the sirens. His Head of Department told him what she knew. When Adam got down to the atrium, there was pandemonium. No one seemed to be in charge or know what to do next. There were no senior staff available to restore order.

He ended up taking Mrs Samson to the hospital, simply because he knew her best. Kath assumed that Kev had got into one of his scrapes and that the doctors would soon patch him up. All the way to the hospital, she chattered about the findings of Independent Police Inquiry into her husband Errol's death. It had at last reached its verdict. The Commissioners' judgement had been in her favour. They accepted that the police let the family down. The custody sergeant had somehow missed the matches that had fallen into the lining of Errol's jacket. She should soon be getting compensation.

Elroy was waiting for them when they reached the desk. His face was ashen. Kev was in intensive care. Kath doubled over in pain and started to scream. She was immediately ushered into a side room with her older son. "Tell Mr Shaw," Elroy ordered, so Adam drove to my house next.

Milo managed to return to work the following September, but he was still traumatised. New Eydon staggered on for another year. The Trust found a succession of Deputies to assist Rhiannon, but none seemed to understand how to reshape children's behaviour. They were blind to the bullying. None found ways of getting to the truth like Secret Friends or getting the parents of pupils in toxic classes around the table. According to Adam, they stayed in their offices, hunched over their computers, preoccupied with budgets and cutbacks.

The last I heard, the three pupils who made up my initial interview panel were all thriving. The one student who keeps in most regular email contact with me is Elroy Samson. Despite all the shocks he suffered, he is on track to become a primary school teacher. Alice Lawton went to Oxford to read English; Noha to the Rocky Mountains with her father.

She hates the Canadian winters, but they have not stopped her following in her grandfather's footsteps and running marathons.

Dr Awad found a job as the Vice Principal at another International School in the Middle East. Maria Telemann, the probationary history teacher who was so deeply respected by her classes, left for Australia with Whiz Wilson. Miss Starr went from strength to strength and the last I heard she had become an Ofsted Inspector.

However, the numbers applying to the New Eydon from the Primary Schools dwindled. Permanent exclusions rocketed. The GCSE results slumped to the bottom of the National League Table. Today, New Eydon's beautiful, copper-sheathed building stands as empty as a shipwreck. A mean business, indeed.

Selected Bibliography

Bidegaray, A.-I. and Pollard, A. M. "Tesserae Recycling in the Production of Medieval Blue Window Glass." Archaeometry, January 2018.

Briant, E., Watson, N. and Philo, G. "Reporting Disability in the Age of Austerity: The Changing Face of Media Representation of Disability and Disabled People in the United Kingdom and the Creation of New 'Folk Devils'." Disability and Society, vol. 28, no. 6, 2013, pp. 874–889.

Brontë, C. Jane Eyre, 1847.

Canter, L. Assertive Discipline, 1993.

Chapman, C. "Ofsted and School Improvement: Teachers' Perceptions of the Inspection Process in Schools Facing Challenging Circumstances." School Leadership and Management, vol. 22, no. 3, 2002, pp. 257–272.

Clark, P. Back from the Brink, Metro Books, 1998.

Coffield F, "Will the Leopard Change its Spots?", UCL Institute of Education Press, 2017

Davies, A. and White, J. "Accountability and School Inspection." Journal of Philosophy of Education, vol. 35, no. 4, 2001, pp. 667–681.

Dooley, M. Letters from Yorkshire

Faruqi, S. "A Culture of Despondency." Education, March 1996, pp 10–11.

Fielding, M. "Ofsted, Inspection and the Betrayal of Democracy." University of Sussex, Falmer, 2008

Fullan, M.G. Successful School Improvement, Open University Press, 1992

Gilroy, P. and Wilcox, B. "Ofsted, Criteria and the Nature of Social Understanding: A Wittgensteinian Critique of the Practice of Educational Judgement." BERA: 2012.

Goleman, D. "What Makes a Leader." More than Sound, 2014

Gray, J. "Frames of Reference and Traditions of Interpretation: Some Issues in the Identification of 'Under-Achieving' Schools." British Journal of Educational Studies, vol. 52, no. 3, 2004, pp. 293–309.

Hay McBer. "A Model of Teacher Effectiveness – A Report by Hay McBer to the DfEE." June 2000.

Hobbes, T. Leviathan, First Avenue Classics, 2018

Huberman, "Introduction", In Fullan, M.G. (ed.) Successful School Improvement, Open University Press, 1992

Lankshear, C. Changing Literacies, Open University Press, 1997.

Lee, J. and Fitz, J. "HMI and Ofsted." British Journal of Educational Studies, vol. 45, no. 1, 1997, pp. 39-52.

MacBeath, J. "Ofsted as a Learning Organisation." Educational Review, vol. 14, no. 2, 2001, pp. 9-12.

McKinney, S. "Poverty Proofing Schools." Researching Education Bulletin, pp. 7-9, June 2016.

Marvell, A. "To a Coy Mistress."

Menendez, R. Stand and Deliver, Scholastic, 1989

Ouston, J., Earley, P. and Fidler, B. Ofsted Inspections, David Fulton, 1996.

Sewell J, Stepping inside the image: a case study in Sacred Space and art. Practical Theology, pp 114-126: 2017

Spielman, A. "SEND Pupils 'Pushed Out of Sight and Out of Mind'." Times Educational Supplement, 10 December 2017

Stubbs, M. Ahead of the Class, John Murray, 2003.

Waller, W. The Sociology of Teaching, Martino Publishing, 2014

Watson, J. "Ofsted's Spiritual Dimension." Cambridge Journal of Education, vol. 31, no. 2, pp.205-219, 2001.

Acknowledgements

My thanks go to perceptive friends and readers: Sally Reynolds, Fahd Khan, Paul Wheeler, Sheila Farnell, John Golds, John Furber, Besan Jaawan, Alice Polwarth and Graham Swift for all their helpful suggestions and encouragement. Responsibility for the finished text rests with me, though.

Thanks especially to Michael Sessions for his support. All proceeds from 'Turbulent School' will be offered to the Friends' School, Ramallah.